ENDORSEMENTS

In *Breaking the Strongholds of Iniquity*, Dr. Bill Dennington bridges the gap between Christ's finished work of redemption on the cross and believers' reception of the fullness of their inheritance and fulfillment of their divine destiny. Knowing that satan is not only a liar, but also a lawyer, Bill clearly reveals and presents remediation for the legal issues surrounding iniquity that keep believers from becoming vessels of honor—fit for the Master's use. I highly recommend this excellent work!

ROBERT J. WINTERS, DMIN
Senior Pastor
Prepare the Way International Church
Phoenix, AZ

I thank God for Dr. Dennington and this excellent teaching that is so needed in this hour in the Body of Christ. Sharing from his own life, Dr. Dennington unpacks the importance of incorporating a biblical understanding of Heaven's legal system into your walk with God. For all those who have questions regarding the Courts of Heaven and whether we need to operate there—this book answers ALL your questions with scriptural clarity!

Furthermore, he provides an exceptional teaching on iniquity and how the enemy uses it as a legal means to frustrate and hinder our walk with God. Without a doubt, the revelation and explanation contained in *Breaking the Strongholds of Iniquity* is a tool that can catapult the Body of Christ into a new dimension of authority.

BEVERLY WATKINS
Johannesburg, South Africa

Breaking the Strongholds of Iniquity is a well-written book by Dr. Bill Dennington concerning your place in the Courts of Heaven and the number-one tactic that satan uses against the church today: Time. I encourage everyone to study this book, develop your spiritual walk with God and begin to take back the things that belong to you. In the deliverance ministry I have seen satan use "time" to steal victory after victory from the saints of God. Let *Breaking the Strongholds of Iniquity* be your guide on entering into the Courts of Heaven and defeating your enemy.

KEITH CHANCEY
Overseer of Norvel Hayes Ministries

In this book the reader will discover many biblical secrets of a believer's dominion! Too many Christians have been delayed, hindered, and denied from enjoying the fruits of what Jesus Christ obtained for them through His death, burial, resurrection, and seating at the right hand of the Father. Today can be the beginning of reversing your losses in life and accumulating victory in every area of your life that seemingly escaped you in the past! I highly recommend that every believer get their own copy of this much-needed tool and read it several times and join in the victory parade!

PASTOR CLYDE OLIVER
Maranatha Christian Center of Melbourne, FL

With thanksgiving I am honored to endorse Bill Dennington's first published book written after many years of successes, trials and tribulations. Rather than tell you about the book that you are about to read, I would like to tell you about the author as I know him.

It has been my privilege to know Bill since he was a young teenager. We attended the same church in Atlanta, Georgia where his mother and I prayed together for our sons. Throughout the years it has been my honor to watch Bill from those early years when his enthusiasm for the Word of God came alive! Bill and Lorie have served in ministry for several years, and I can share about this couple from a close-up view of their walk of faith. Lorie is Bill's number-one (1) intercessor. Bill is a student of the Bible. He has remained teachable and teaches others from a heart of love for God and people. He and Lorie have climbed the mountaintops where they experienced the glory of God, and they have walked through deep, dark valleys of despair. They never gave up; they continued to seek God, the giver of life! I encourage you to read this insightful book written by a man who talks the talk and walks the walk!

GERMAINE GRIFFIN COPELAND
Best-selling author of the *Prayers That Avail Much* book series
Greensboro, Georgia

Breaking *the* STRONGHOLDS *of* INIQUITY

A New Testament Guide to Cleansing
Your Generational Bloodline

BILL DENNINGTON
with Robert Henderson

DESTINY IMAGE® PUBLISHERS, INC.

P.O. Box 310, Shippensburg, PA 17257-0310

"Promoting Inspired Lives."

This book and all other Destiny Image and Destiny Image Fiction books are available at Christian bookstores and distributors worldwide.

Cover design by Eileen Rockwell

Interior design by Terry Clifton

For more information on foreign distributors, call 717-532-3040.

Reach us on the Internet: www.destinyimage.com.

ISBN 13 TP: 978-0-7684-5265-5

ISBN 13 eBook: 978-0-7684-5266-2

ISBN 13 HC: 978-0-7684-5268-6

ISBN 13 LP: 978-0-7684-5267-9

For Worldwide Distribution, Printed in the U.S.A.

3 4 5 6 7 8 / 24 23 22 21 20

DEDICATION

To my beloved wife, Lorie, who has stood with me and believed in me for so many years. Your faith in Jesus, and in me, has been such an inspiration and strength! Thank you for your encouragement and love! Without you and your faithful support, this, my first of many books to come, would still be an impossible dream. Thank you! I love you!

ACKNOWLEDGMENTS

No one in the Body of Christ is self-made. And there is no fruit in ministry apart from the people who help and assist along the way. I want to acknowledge at least some of the people who inspired and encouraged me in the run-up to the production of this book.

I must give credit to the vast majority of understanding and insight that led to the writing of this work, Robert Henderson. Thank you, sir, for your faithfulness to the Lord to give birth to the revelation of the Courts of Heaven. Thank you for your apostolic leadership, which set things in order for my church, my ministry, my family, and my life. And thank you for believing in me to the point that you would allow me the honor of helping you to herald the message of the Courts of Heaven with your personal endorsement.

I want to thank my spiritual parents, Kenneth and Gloria Copeland, for bringing me up as a true son in the faith. Your lives and testimony of faith still set the standard of excellence that I endeavor to reach and maintain every day.

I offer my heartfelt gratitude to the Global Reformers HUB leaders for your complete acceptance and fullhearted endorsement to write this book. That day in Branson, Missouri, will always be a day of remembrance and encouragement!

I give thanks for the partners and members of Harvestfire Church International for your love, support, and encouragement. You make being in the ministry a joy and something to celebrate each and every day!

I can't leave out my family! My son, Grant, and his amazing wife, Rachel; my daughter, Lindsay, and her outstanding husband, Kelsey; and my growing group of grandchildren, all have contributed to the success of what God has called me to do, this book being only one tiny part of that calling.

Finally, I want to give my eternal thanks and praise to Jesus, my Lord, the Righteous Judge, who lives in constant fellowship with me and loves me like no one else ever has or ever could!

CONTENTS

FOREWORD

I first met Bill and Lorie Dennington in 1978. In the years since then we have become more than good friends. I have laughed with them in good times and ministered to Bill and his whole family when his young grandson unexpectedly died at the age of two years old.

Rather than grieving and accusing God for this terrible tragedy, I watched as Bill led his entire family to absolute victory in Christ Jesus. The whole family stood on the Word of the living God and practiced what Bill has preached all his ministry life: the Word of faith.

Preaching is one thing; living it is another. Bill and his family demonstrated what it means to be vessels of honor as in Second Timothy 2:20-21.

The Dennington family could have chosen to blame God and grieve until the spirit of grief and sorrow—the devil—entered their lives and continued to steal, kill, and destroy. But instead, they chose to make their stand until the joy of the Lord manifested, which became their strength.

Why is this so important? Throughout this book, by the Spirit of divine revelation, Bill will introduce to so many, for the first time, the Courts of Heaven and how Jesus, our heavenly judge, functions.

There is a legal side and a vital, or living, side to our redemption. Bill helped open my spiritual eyes to the legal side. One must have working knowledge of both in order to enjoy, to the fullest, the victory declared in First Corinthians 15:57: *"But thanks be to God, which giveth us the victory through our Lord Jesus Christ"* (KJV).

Study this book along with your Bible. Don't just take Brother Dennington's word for it. As you'll see, the Word of God, the Bible, is his final authority. You and all yours will be glad you did!

JESUS IS LORD!
KENNETH COPELAND

INTRODUCTION

At the time of this writing, I have been in the ministry for forty years. Twenty-seven of those year have been in pastoral ministry; twenty-six years of those as a senior pastor. In that time you get to experience a lot in the realm of prayer. You also get to observe a lot of varied results in the lives of the people you are responsible to lead and teach in the ways of the Kingdom of God.

I have seen and experienced a lot of victories. I have also seen and experienced a fair number of situations that did not turn out according to expectations. This can set people up for disappointment, especially when they believed they were doing everything according to what they were taught.

Now, I understand that there are a lot of unknown variables in the process. Did I communicate clearly and accurately? Was what I communicated heard and understood? Was the truth that was taught acted upon in agreement with spiritual laws and principles? The questions may seem endless, but in the passionate desire to see God's people live a life of victory, those questions must be asked and answered.

One reality that must be considered is that we don't live our life of faith in a vacuum. We are spiritual beings living in a physical environment that is largely being influenced by activity in the realm of the spirit. The Bible makes it clear we have an enemy, and he and his demonic forces have a clearly defined agenda. Jesus identified that agenda in John 10:10:

> *The thief does not come except to steal, and to kill, and to destroy. I have come that they may have life, and that they may have it more abundantly.*

If you are reading this book, you are more than likely desiring to enjoy the life that Jesus has to offer and find a way to eliminate as much as possible the ability of the thief to successfully carry out his agenda against you and your family. It is probably evident that there is a conflict, maybe even a war, that is taking place at times that makes living this life a challenge. It should be obvious that when attempting to live out salvation in real time there are some things that are not automatic where success and victory are concerned.

What Jesus accomplished when He died on the cross, and ultimately was raised from the dead and ascended to the right hand of the Father to put into effect, did not stop the conflict! All you have to do is read the Book of Acts, and the letters of the New Testament to discover that, if anything, the conflict became more intense.

We must be careful not to dismiss the reality of satan's ability to carry out strategies of his design, that if left unchallenged, will produce much heartache and destruction. Believers must never let their guard down and always live their lives with an awareness that the enemy is constantly seeking an opportunity to hinder, delay, and even destroy their life, family and future.

In the 1990s the concept of spiritual warfare was introduced to the Body of Christ, and it was a needed revelation. Many became aware of the enemy for the first time and began to wake up to the need to position themselves in a place of spiritual resistance against the devil's strategies and tactics that hinder the Kingdom of God in the earth. Great victories were won, and great progress was gained in individual lives and on a corporate level within the Body of Christ.

Over the past ten to fifteen years, the results of the efforts to resist demonic powers and stop the encroachment of destructive attacks in individual lives, and even against churches and ministries, did not garner the same results as in the initial years of walking in the light of the revelation about spiritual warfare.

It seemed as if the enemy had found a way to keep the upper hand in many situations. One thing that I saw taking place repeatedly was that time was being used as a weapon against God's people and time would run out before the manifestation of victory could be secured. Tragedy and destruction and disappointment were the result on an ever-increasing basis too.

Even in my own life, family, and ministry there were attacks of the enemy and circumstances that were connected to what the Bible clearly states are manifestations of the curse that previously had responded to my resistance through faith, but in recent times I began to notice were not being defeated as quickly as I had seen in the past. And in some cases these things were not responding at all. Time was passing and nothing was changing. In fact, in some cases, things were getting worse.

The result of this delay is deferred hope. Proverbs 13:12 reveals this clearly: *"Hope deferred makes the heart sick, but when the desire comes, it is a tree of life."*

This is what the enemy is after. He is a master at extending the battle with the motive to wear believers out and put pressure on them to make them give up and quit.

> *He will speak out against the Most High and wear down the saints of the Highest One, and he will intend to make alterations in times and in law; and they will be given into his hand for a time, times, and half a time* (Daniel 7:25 NASB).

This verse is speaking of the antichrist, but we know from First John 4:3 the spirit of antichrist is already operating in the world even now. That spirit is, of course, satan himself. His intention is to interfere with things to such an extent that he can wear down God's people. And we see this happening more and more in our day.

However, there is a way to defeat this kind of strategy, and it is revealed in Daniel 7:26:

But the court shall be seated, and they shall take away his dominion, to consume and destroy it forever.

While this is again referring to the time of the actual anti-christ, Daniel had already seen this in a vision:

I watched till thrones were put in place, and the Ancient of Days was seated; His garment was white as snow, and the hair of His head was like pure wool. His throne was a fiery flame, its wheels a burning fire; a fiery stream issued and came forth from before Him. A thousand thousands ministered to Him; ten thousand times ten thousand stood before Him. The court was seated, and the books were opened (Daniel 7:9-10).

Notice the very last sentence in verse 10: "*The court was seated, and the books were opened.*" This confirms that there is a heavenly court. It also reveals that there are books that contain legal aspects of God's plans and purposes that are opened when the court is in session.

In Luke 18:1-8 Jesus introduced a level of prayer that involved dealing with a situation where the only way to get results is to approach God as a judge who could bring speedy vengeance from a legal maneuver by an adversary. I will deal with this more later in the book, but it is important to understand that our conflict is not just one that takes place in a battlefield; it is also one that can play out in the Court of Heaven.

In the pages of this book you will learn about many of the ways that the devil has used to delay, hinder, and even deny the results we have been believing for when we exercise our faith and seek results in prayer. You will begin to understand that if the adversary has found something legal in nature with which to hinder God's will or purpose in your life, you will not be able to get that situation changed on the battlefield. You will learn that there is another arena where by faith you can step into to secure your already purchased and promised victory. This arena is the Courts of Heaven.

I learned about this from Robert Henderson. Robert and I have become personal friends and associates in ministry, and much of what I share in this book I learned from him. He will offer some insights in a chapter in this book as well, and I am deeply grateful for his wisdom and leadership.

The focus of this book is one of the main things that the adversary uses against us that is of a legal nature. This would be bloodline iniquity. I will define iniquity in the early chapters of this book. I will also share how to remove iniquity, even that which has passed from previous generations of your family, and stop generational curses and behavior that can be destructive and even deadly. I will also show, from a New Testament perspective, why we are responsible for cleansing our bloodlines of iniquity and why this is necessary.

This is not just theory. Robert and I, as well as a multitude of other people, have found freedom and deliverance by going before Jesus as the Righteous Judge in the Courts of Heaven. It has worked to free families from the legal things that kept generational curses in place and were the source of so much defeat and destruction. Learning to step by faith into the Courts of Heaven is a powerful strategy when the situation calls for it, and it is extremely effective. It isn't hard to learn or to implement because we are actually already positioned as born-again believers in that courtroom where everything is provided for us to win every case!

One last thing I want to share with you as we begin this journey into the Courts of Heaven. I have been totally immersed in studying and tearing into the guts of this revelation for better than two and a half years at the time I am writing this. I have researched, investigated, and questioned everything about this subject. Having been a student of the Word of God for forty-two years and having earned postgraduate degrees in theology before being introduced to this revelation, I had every reason to make sure that this is biblically sound from a New Testament perspective. I had to ensure that the revelation of the Courts of Heaven was sound theologically and doctrinally and that it aligned with the revelation of Jesus Christ from a new covenant perspective. I also had to prove for myself that it produced results that were proof of the Holy Spirit and the power of God.

I am more convinced today than ever before that this agrees with the New Testament revelation of the finished work of redemption. The Courts of Heaven and the understanding of how to go before Jesus as the Righteous Judge has opened so many dimensions of what Jesus secured for us at Calvary and how to appropriate it that it is astounding to me.

Questions I have been asking for more than forty-two years of Christian living, that had not been answered for years, are being answered and giving me understanding as to why certain things took place in my life in a way that were not in agreement with the expectation that faith and grace had caused me to expect. So many other people, including members of my family and church as well as other ministers and believers, had questions about situations and circumstances in their lives that just didn't make sense in the light of what we all had been taught and believed should take place when we exercise authority or resist the devil by faith. I have come to understand that what we have been taught and believed was not wrong, it was just incomplete.

That is no fault of those who taught us; it is the simple truth that there are certain revelations that cannot be brought forth in any amount of fullness until the Body of Christ comes to the place that they have ears to hear and eyes to see what God wants them to receive. Maturity is a prerequisite for greater dimensions of truth to be revealed.

If you truly want to have many of your questions answered about why your prayers may have not been effective and things in certain areas of your life or family have been such a struggle, follow along with me through the pages of this book and have your eyes opened to this powerful dimension of the Courts of Heaven and learn how to function there by faith to remove generational issues from your life and family forever!

Chapter 1

THE FINISHED WORK
OF REDEMPTION

In 1977, not long after I was born again and filled with the Holy Spirit, someone gave me a set of books by E. W. Kenyon. These books were to become a major part of my spiritual foundation as I learned about what I have come to describe "in Christ realities."

Knowing who you are in Christ and who He is in you as a believer is an absolutely vital revelation that you must renew your mind to if you ever intend on living a life of victory. What God did in Christ and through Christ—for all who would receive Him as Lord—is one of the most powerful things you could ever learn to encourage a life of faith that refuses to accept defeat.

All these many years later I find myself going back to these fundamental New Testament truths revealed through the letters of the New Testament. The revelation of the Courts of Heaven and our right, privilege, and responsibility to function there is such a major dimension of the believer's life of victory that I find it difficult to express it!

Kenyon shared two major revelations from the New Testament that are keys to understanding both why the Courts of Heaven exist and how to take advantage of the power of the court to gain advantage over the strategies of the devil when you run into unyielding resistance from him in any given situation.

The first of these truths is substitution and identification; and the second one is the legal and vital side of redemption. These two powerful revelations open up for the believer the key to understanding all that Jesus Christ accomplished in His suffering, death, resurrection, and ascension, which is known as the finished work of redemption.

The finished work of redemption was the greatest legal transaction that was ever accomplished in the history of Creation. Jesus fulfilled the Law of Moses in its entirety; satisfying every legal demand the Law called for where the judging of sin and the sinner was concerned.

The second person of the Godhead took on a body, legally, through the virgin birth and lived here as a man. He is called the Last Adam. Jesus Himself referred to Himself as the "Son of Man." This is important to acknowledge because the only way the Law could be satisfied fully is for a man to be offered up for Adam's sin, and it had to be a perfect man at that. Jesus qualified for He was sinless by having no iniquity in His blood. His blood came from His Father, who was God Himself!

Second Corinthians 5:19 states, *"God was in Christ reconciling the world to Himself."* In other words, God took it upon Himself to open the way for men to be joined back to God spiritually, and Jesus Christ, His Son, was the way He accomplished this. Jesus was 100 percent God and 100 percent man; this enabled Him to be an acceptable sacrifice that forever satisfied the eternal courts of justice and the Law of God that demanded justice for Adam's high treason.

His blood did not just cover man's sin; it remitted it, totally removing it as a barrier between God and man. Second Corinthians 5:19 goes on to state, *"God was in Christ reconciling the world to Himself, not imputing their trespasses to them."*

The apostle Paul quotes a powerful passage from Psalm 32 in Romans 4:6-8:

> *David also describes the blessedness of the man to whom God imputes righteousness apart from works: "Blessed are those whose lawless deeds are forgiven, and whose sins are covered; blessed is the man to whom the Lord shall not impute sin."*

As a result of what Jesus did, the entire world has been blessed by God in that He has accepted Jesus's sacrifice as efficacious enough to forever remit the effects of Adam's iniquity in the Garden of Eden so that mankind can make the choice to enter back into union with God through acceptance of Jesus as their Lord through faith. But that was not all that Jesus accomplished!

He not only dealt with Adam's sin and all other sin his iniquity gave birth to; Jesus also dealt with the resulting effects of that iniquity, which was the legal right for the curse to begin to afflict mankind. Through the curse satan had gained the right to legally accomplish his goal of stealing, killing, and destroying. He isn't satisfied to just go after mankind; he wants to corrupt the entire creation under man's dominion too.

We can see several things afflicted Adam and Eve in the Garden of Eden after sin occurred. Spiritual death, which is separation from God as the primary and sole source for everything, lodged in Adam's and Eve's spirit. Because of sin they stepped out of experiencing the life of God and stepped into a life now lived in union with spiritual death whose source was the Lord of death, the devil. This led to a terrible series of manifestations of the curse that still afflicts mankind today.

Fear, poverty, lack, sickness, disease, and physical death all are the offspring of the spiritual death that became man's inheritance from Adam. Iniquity, the infection that passed on to all mankind from the head of the human race, put all men into the realm of death and under the legal right of the devil to afflict mankind and the earth with the curse.

Romans 5:12-14 explains this inheritance of sin very plainly:

> *When Adam sinned, the entire world was affected. Sin entered human experience, and death was the result. And so death followed this sin, casting its shadow over all humanity, because all have sinned.*

Sin was in the world before Moses gave the written law, but it was not charged against them where no law existed. Yet death reigned as king from Adam to Moses even though they hadn't broken a command the way Adam had. The first man, Adam, was a picture of the Messiah, who was to come (TPT).

What we see working here is what Romans 8:2 calls *"the law of sin and death."* This is a spiritual law that Adam put into motion and set as the governing spiritual law over all mankind. Even though God could not hold men responsible for their sin because the Law of Moses had not been given, the result of sin, which is death, was working its deadly work from Adam to Moses. It was what men inherited by having Adam's DNA.

Dr. Brian Simmons, author of *The Passion Translation*, has a note on the last sentence of Romans 5:14: "The actions of both Adam and Christ affect the entire world. Death passes to all who are in Adam; life passes to all who are in Christ. Each is a corporate head of a race of people. God sees every person as in Adam or in Christ."[1]

This is such a powerful statement that reveals the absolute necessity to receive Jesus as Lord, for without disconnecting from Adam and joining yourself to Christ you have no legal inheritance to anything that God has provided through the finished work of redemption. Just being a "good person" is not going to disconnect you from Adam spiritually. Neither is perfect obedience to the Law of Moses going to remove you from Adam's race spiritually. Only faith in Jesus Christ and receiving Him as your Lord moves you spiritually and legally from Adam's inheritance of sin and spiritual death into Christ's inheritance of eternal life.

There are essentially only two families in the earth today. You can read First John 3:10 and see that there is the family of God and the family of the devil. Jesus identified the religious people of His day in John 8:44 as having the devil as their father. Jesus identified His Father as God and explained to Nicodemus in John 3:3 that we must be born from above.

I like a word that is used to refer to being born again that is found in Clarence Jordon's rendering of First Peter 1:22: *"For you all have been refathered, not by a mortal man, but by the immortal word of a living and abiding God."*[2] To be "born again" is to literally be "refathered" from above!

To change families you must change fathers. The law of fatherhood is a law that is revealed quite clearly throughout the Bible, and it does determine your inheritance, earthly, physically, and spiritually.

Even though God legally took care of the spiritual hindrances on His side of the ledger that was keeping Him and mankind separated, it does not happen automatically. It only becomes a vital, living reality spiritually in the life of a man, woman, or child when he or she accepts Jesus as his or her Lord. It is then, and only then, that that person is "born again" and is translated out of Adam's race and into the race of God-men who are spiritually one with God through union with Christ!

Jesus, as a second Adam, became our substitute and identified with Adam's race on the cross. He took Adam's sin and bore it and suffered the same fate it rendered unto Adam, which was spiritual death. Only Jesus did what He did as a sacrifice and in obedience to His Father, rather than in an act of self-willed disobedience as Adam had done.

At the same time, Jesus bore all the legal effects of sin in His soul and body. He suffered the oppression of fear; He bore the brunt of all sickness and disease; He became completely impoverished spiritually and physically all the way up to and including becoming the curse itself and legally bearing it for He was made to be sin on that cross (see Isa. 53; Matt. 8:17; 2 Cor. 5:21; Gal. 3:13; 1 Pet. 2:24).

When we are born-again through faith in Jesus, we iden-tify with Him as He is now, for we are one spirit with Him (see 1 Cor. 6:17; 1 John 4:17). This is the powerful truth of substitution and identification! Jesus became everything we were through our union with Adam, so that we could become everything He is now through union with Him and the Father!

The new birth is what opens the door to what was estab-lished as a legal right in the mind of God for all mankind through the finished work of redemption. It is what enables the legal right to become a living reality in the life of the one who is born again! It is this legal right of inheritance that the devil seeks to challenge; this is why the Court of Heaven is avail-able to the believer to access when any legal claim is made by the enemy in an attempt to deny any part of that inheritance.

We must understand what legal things the devil seeks to use to bring as an accusation or lawsuit with a view to deny, delay, or if possible, destroy our ability to walk in any dimension of our inheritance in Christ in this earth. He can't stop the spiritual side of the inheritance; that was secured through the new birth and the believer becoming a new creation through union with Christ. But the adversary does have ways to deter and deny us of our earthly right to experience our inheritance.

In the pages of this book you will learn some of the key things that the devil uses in a legal manner to try and stop us from enjoying the fullness of our inheritance in Christ while we are living our lives out in the earth. We will also prove, primarily from the New Testament, why those legal things have to be dealt with by the born-again believer in a proper manner.

Spiritual warfare has its place. There are times the enemy will attack, and it is purely out of his hatred of those who are spiritually in union with Christ. In those times, the exercise of our authority and properly using our spiritual weapons will ultimately defeat satan's attack.

But too many times, and I might add all too frequently in recent times, even strong people of faith in God's Word succumb to the deadly effects of sickness and disease. They fight seemingly endless losing battles with addictions and habitual sins. They labor under the crushing pressure of financial lack. Their marriages are breaking up. They fall into the darkness of depression; some even commit suicide when all hope seems lost. All of this is taking place when it seems nothing is changing the situation.

I've witnessed the frustration of pastors, church and family members, and so many other believers who were standing in faith and doing everything they knew to do and had been taught to do with nothing turning the tide; they stood not just hours or days and weeks, but months and years. It seemed that time was turned into a weapon and it was a race to find a solution or obtain deliverance. Sadly too many have been losing the race. This is unacceptable!

In many of the cases I am personally close to and know the intimate details, I can honestly say that the people who were losing the battle lived out their understanding of faith all the way to the end. They believed the Word, confessed the Word, took communion, refused to speak doubt or words of fear. They were faithful to support their church and favorite ministries financially. Yet, the situation did not turn in their favor.

The accusation that they did not have enough faith is, frankly, unjust. These were not spiritually lazy people. Many I am reflecting on were longtime seasoned ministers who preached and taught faith. Some were known for their own ministry where thousands received through miracles, deliverance, and healing through prayers of faith.

There is one thing that I am learning that could have been at the root of the problem. Our enemy engages us in a spiritual battlefield and is operating as a thief all the time. Our enemy is operating against us as a thief all the time; he also attacks us using strategies carried out as if on a spiritual battlefield as well.

But, he can also operate against us as one who seeks to bring lawsuits against us. He can and will search out legal things and present cases make accusations against us in a very real Court of Heaven. When he uses this strategy, you will not defeat him with spiritual warfare like a king on a battlefield. You will have to step by faith into the Court of Heaven and engage that strategy as a priest and remove the legal things, taking full advantage of the legal side of the finished work of redemption.

The reality of the judicially legal side of the realm of the spirit is something that we must awaken to if we are to expand the influence of the Kingdom of God in the earth effectively. Everything in the realm of the spirit is legal in nature, and God cannot pervert justice. When it comes to enforcing the powerful results of the redemptive work in Jesus's death, burial, resurrection, and ascension in the earth, nothing is automatic.

I will return to this facet of redemption later in this book, but first we need to gain a basic understanding of the things that comprise the legal issues that our enemy can use to stop God's prophetic destiny being fulfilled in our lives, cities, states, regions, and nations. The primary thing we need to learn about is something the Bible calls "iniquity."

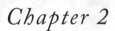

Chapter 2

THE ROOTS OF INIQUITY

When God created Adam and put him in the Garden of Eden, the spiritual environment that existed in this earth was already hostile to Adam's existence. An enemy was already observing the creation of man and began to forge a plan to bring him down.

This spiritual being who sought to overcome Adam had, at one time in the past, held a place of rulership over the earth and had access to Heaven's court. He had been cast out of Heaven and now occupied a place in the spirit that was subservient to mankind as of the result of the dominion mandate God Himself gave Adam (see Gen. 1:28; Ps. 8:4-6). With Adam given this mandate and fulfilling it, this being once called lucifer and now called satan saw that even his place in the earth was now threatened.

It is important to investigate some biblical records as to the history pertaining to satan's past. This is important information that gives us insight into why we must always be on guard and as Peter wrote, we must *"be sober, be vigilant; because your adversary the devil walks about like a roaring lion, seeking who he may devour"* (1 Pet. 5:8).

One day as I was studying on the Courts of Heaven, the Lord spoke to me and said, "You need to do a study on iniquity to learn of its beginnings and how it manifested when it was discovered." So, I did. I was amazed at what I found out as I researched the Scriptures where this was concerned!

My study led me to a time in the past (as revealed through the Old Testament prophetic writings) when lucifer held a high and lofty position in the Kingdom of God. Let's look at Ezekiel 28.

In verses 1 through 10 we find that the Lord is addressing the "prince of Tyre" who was in fact the man who was the ruler of this ancient city. He was actually an under-ruler, an earthly king who was a spiritual prince functioning under the direct influence of a ruling spirit who controlled his place of government.

This ruling spirit had influenced the man to think that he was a god and functioned from a place of government (a seat) in the realm of the spirit. He possessed a wisdom that exceeded Daniel's wisdom, but his wisdom was derived from the spiritual overlord who had virtually possessed this man who was allowing this entity to have full expression through him.

This entity was actually lucifer who is now the one we know of as satan, or the devil. The prince of Tyre was yielding himself to the influence of satan, granting him a great measure of expression in the earth through this earthly ruler's governmental position.

God proclaims a judgment against this earthly ruler of Tyre, and the verdict was death by the sword. He would find out that he was not a god, but a man, and he would die at the hands of an army of an invading nation.

God then speaks to the devil and calls him the "king of Tyre," indicating that he was the true ruler of Tyre. God goes on to rehearse his history from the ages past and we will look a just a few of these verses.

> *Son of man, take up a lamentation for the king of Tyre, and say to him, "Thus says the Lord God: 'You were the seal of perfection, full of wisdom and perfect in beauty. You were in Eden, the garden of God; every precious stone was your covering....You were the anointed cherub who covers; I established you; you were on the holy mountain of God; you walked back and forth in the midst of fiery stones. You were perfect in your ways from the day you were created, till iniquity was found in you"* (Ezekial 28:12-15).

As an anointed cherub he was created perfect. He was the sum of wisdom and extremely beautiful. He had a place of function in God's government and conducted business on the heavenly trading floors where the fiery stones are located in the Court of Heaven before the throne of God.

Lucifer did as he was supposed to do in his place of responsibility in the government and economy of the Kingdom of God until iniquity was found in his heart. Let's look at Isaiah 14 and take note of something revealed in verses 12 through 15.

> *How you are fallen from heaven, O Lucifer, son of the morning! How you are cut down to the ground, You who weakened the nations! For you have said in your heart: "I will ascend into heaven, I will exalt my throne above the stars of God; I will also sit on the mount of the congregation on the farthest sides of the north; I will ascend above the heights of the clouds, I will be like the Most High." Yet you shall be brought down to Sheol, to the lowest depths of the Pit.*

Iniquity showed up within lucifer's heart by what is revealed in verses 13 and 14. He was exercising self-will in rebellion to God's will. There are five self-willed declarations of lucifer's intentions that set him on a course of attempting a heavenly coup.

This is the first time iniquity showed up in the history of Heaven. In the heart of one of the lead angels in the Kingdom of God; the one who was charged with the responsibility of stewarding the worship of God on the trading floors of Heaven. And it cost lucifer his heavenly seat.

Jesus said in Luke 10:18, *"I saw Satan as lightning fall from heaven."* As second person of the Godhead, Jesus would have witnessed this expulsion, and most probably was the One who executed the verdict and judgment against satan. This is even recorded in some detail in Revelation 12:7-10:

> *And war broke out in heaven: Michael and his angels fought with the dragon; and the dragon and his angels fought, but they did not prevail, nor was a place found for them in heaven any longer. So the great dragon was cast out, that serpent of old, called the Devil and Satan, who deceives the whole world; he was cast to the earth, and his angels were cast out with him. Then I heard a loud voice saying in heaven, "Now salvation, and strength, and the kingdom of our God, and the power of His Christ have come, for the accuser of our brethren, who accused them before our God day and night, has been cast down."*

This is a record of something that has already taken place in the past. (Bible prophecy can not only speak to the future; it can also reveal things of the past that have impact on the future.) When lucifer corrupted himself through iniquity and became satan, he also influenced the angels who were under his authority to attempt an overthrow of the Kingdom of God and did not succeed. They all were cast out of Heaven and banished to the earth which had been under lucifer's stewardship and government. This event is what had already taken place prior to Adam's creation in the Garden of Eden.

God told Adam that he would have to exercise dominion and do this as He put him in the Garden of Eden to cultivate it and guard it (see Gen. 2:15). You don't need to exercise dominion over something or guard something if there is no enemy already present.

There is no record of the time that passed while Adam and his wife were in the Garden as this enemy observed their activities. One reason this is so is because time was not an issue or concern to man prior to his fall. He was an eternal being, created by God to live forever. Time had no dominion over him up until he fell through sin and became a mortal being subject to death. We must assume that satan had to take some measured and careful observation of man and his activities and watch for any tendencies that could potentially give an opportunity to move in and walk *"about like a roaring lion, seeking whom he may devour"* (1 Pet. 5:8).

We can read what took place eventually, after the devil determined his best strategy to devour what was the head of all mankind. Let's read this story from Genesis 3:1-6:

> *Now the serpent was more cunning than any beast of the field which the Lord God had made. And he said to the woman, "Has God indeed said, 'You shall not eat of every tree of the garden'?" And the woman said to the serpent, "We may eat the fruit of the trees of the garden; but of the fruit of the tree which is in the midst of the garden, God has said, 'You shall not eat it, nor shall you touch it, lest you die.'" Then the serpent said to the woman, "You will not surely die. For*

God knows that in the day you eat of it your eyes will be opened, and you will be like God, knowing good and evil." So when the woman saw that the tree was good for food, that it was pleasant to the eyes, and a tree desirable to make one wise, she took of its fruit and ate. She also gave to her husband with her, and he ate.

At this point in this story we need to refer to some insight given in First Timothy 2:14, *"Adam was not deceived, but the woman being deceived, fell into transgression."* This is an extremely important insight. Adam, the head of the human race, did not fall into transgression by deception. He willfully stepped into sin with his eyes wide open. He committed iniquity.

He could have inquired of the Lord as to how to handle this entire situation even before the woman was influenced to take that first bite. But he didn't. As an act of self-will, he joined her in the act; and as a result, doomed the entire race of man to a life now locked into spiritual death, subject to fear, sickness and disease, poverty and lack, and physical death.

In his spirit Adam was no longer drawing his life force from God; he had stepped into spiritual death, which is spiritual separation from God. He stepped out of light and into darkness. He stepped out of an environment saturated with God's love and was now the object of satan's hatred. Where he once walked in faith toward God, he was now living in fear of God and hid himself from God. But this was because he had lost his original clothing, which emanated from within himself, which was the glory, and attempted to cover his now naked body with fig leaves.

The depths to which man fell was not immediately evident in those first few moments. But the results of that moment still are influencing mankind even to this day.

What Adam and Eve did on that day violated certain unchangeable spiritual laws, and the fruit of those broken laws began to play out over time. A spiritual entity that had no right before man's sin to have a say-so or authority over man's life and destiny had been granted that right; it was a legal position that was established by the self-willed decision of Adam. Romans 5:12 describes the problem; a couple of versions make this really plain to understand:

> *Sin made its entry into the world through one man, and through sin, death. The entail of sin and death passed on to the whole human race, and no one could break it for no one was himself free from sin* (PNT).
>
> *When Adam sinned, the entire world was affected. Sin entered human experience, and death was the result. And so death followed this sin, casting its shadow over all humanity, because all have sinned* (TPT).

An interesting note from A. S. Worrell's translation of the New Testament on this verse: *"Adam was the head of our race: and all his posterity was involved in his sin, and poisoned by it."*[3] This is in perfect agreement with the note I shared from Dr. Brian Simmons on this verse from *The Passion Translation* that

I will repeat for you again: "The actions of both Adam and Christ affect the entire world. Death passes to all who are in Adam; life passes to all who are in Christ. Each is a corporate head of a race of people. God sees every person as in Adam or in Christ."[4]

I want to emphasize this point because of its importance to what we are dealing with in the Courts of Heaven. We came into this life by birth with an inheritance that is legal in nature and affects our spiritual destiny. And this inheritance is established through the bloodline of our family, which ultimately traces all the way back to Adam. This is true no matter where, when, or from whom you were born, and it does affect and shape our lives in ways that are profoundly serious in nature.

In his message to the city of Athens from Mars Hill, the apostle Paul verifies this bloodline inheritance. Look at this passage from Acts 17:24-26:

> *God, who made the world and everything in it, since He is Lord of heaven and earth, does not dwell in temples made with hands. Nor is He worshiped with men's hands, as though He needed anything, since He gives to all life, breath, and all things. And He has made from one blood every nation of men to dwell on all the face of the earth, and has determined their pre-appointed times and the boundaries of their dwellings.*

Many translations reflect that the word *blood* is not found in many of the best Greek texts, but this does not reflect a change in the idea that the entire human family descend from

Adam. Again, quoting a note on verse 26 from Worrell's New Testament, "He made of one blood; one family. All men of all races… trace back to Adam."[5]

From a scientific standpoint, if we had a sample of Adam's DNA, we would unquestionably find a percentage of his DNA in our blood. We all, every man, woman, and child carry in our bodies the genetic markers of the first man, Adam.

Throughout this book I will emphasize a critical theological, doctrinal reality that is a cornerstone of everything pertaining to our identity in Christ. When you and I were born-again, we became a new creation in Christ Jesus. Even though our physical bodies are still "in Adam" as far as its generational history is concerned, our human spirits are no longer connected to Adam's fallen race. We are in Christ, of Christ, and by Christ! You and I do not identify with Adam; we identify with Jesus Christ. All of the old state and condition of our spirit being has changed and has be reborn in the image of Christ. Christ is our pattern, and we measure from our position in Him.

It is this revelation of being in Christ that we must renew our minds to and deal with any issues that relate to our physical bodies. I will be repeatedly emphasizing the need to renew our minds to the reality of who we are in Christ and the need to bring this physical body and its passions and desires into submission to our spirit. Quite frankly, if you are not going to approach the subject of the Courts of Heaven with your position in Christ as the preeminent focus of your identity, you will struggle to get results, because the Courts of Heaven depends on the believer having their identity established in the righteousness and oneness with the Lord Jesus Christ.

So, understanding this, what does this mean as far as our need to learn to go to the Courts of Heaven? How, and to what extent, did the finished work of redemption through Christ Jesus's death, burial, resurrection, and ascension change the way a born-again believer can deal with that part of our physical inheritance? What is different for the believer as a result of becoming the new creation of Second Corinthians 5:17? We will begin to investigate this in the next chapters.

Chapter 3

THE LEGALITY
OF BLOOD

Christianity has both its beginnings and roots in what is essentially an Eastern culture that dates back to antiquity. Much of the basis of the Eastern mind-set is rooted in the importance of blood and the legal strength of blood covenants. This mind-set and understanding has largely been diluted and lost its influence as Christianity spread westward.

The basis of a blood covenant is something that has almost entirely been lost to the "civilized" cultures of the world. We have replaced blood with ink, and a contract's strength is usually determined by how well it can stand up to a legal challenge. Not so with a blood covenant.

The ancient cultures understood the power and importance of blood. Blood was considered to have a spiritual aspect to it. Blood was not just thought of as a conveyer of life, but life itself.

Even in the Book of Genesis God communicated the importance of blood. Look at Genesis 9:4-6:

> *But you shall not eat flesh with its life, that is, its blood. Surely for your lifeblood I will demand a reckoning; from the hand of every beast I will require it, and from the hand of man. From the hand of every man's brother I will require the life of man. Whoever sheds man's blood, by man his blood shall be shed; for in the image of God He made man.*

The shedding of blood unjustly is a legal issue in the realm of the spirit. What we just read was spoken by God long before the giving of the Law of Moses. However, let's consider what the Lord said in Leviticus 17:11, *"For the life of the flesh is in the blood, and I have given it to you upon the altar to make atonement for your souls; for it is the blood that makes atonement for the soul."*

This reveals that blood has the ability to make atonement for a man's soul. This word *atonement* is *kaphar* in Hebrew. The definition of this word is interesting in that it implies that blood is an instrument to be used in a legal manner where a crime, offense, or sin is concerned.

Just because our modern cultures have lost the importance of blood from a spiritual perspective doesn't mean the blood itself has lost that dimension. Blood is still a legal thing in the realm of the spirit.

This is confirmed in the story of the murder of Abel by the hand of his brother Cain found in Genesis 4:1-12:

Now Adam knew Eve his wife, and she conceived and bore Cain, and said, "I have acquired a man from the Lord." Then she bore again, this time his brother Abel. Now Abel was a keeper of sheep, but Cain was a tiller of the ground. And in the process of time it came to pass that Cain brought an offering of the fruit of the ground to the Lord. Abel also brought of the firstborn of his flock and of their fat. And the Lord respected Abel and his offering, but He did not respect Cain and his offering. And Cain was very angry, and his countenance fell. So the Lord said to Cain, "Why are you angry? And why has your countenance fallen? If you do well, will you not be accepted? And if you do not do well, sin lies at the door. And its desire is for you, but you should rule over it." Now Cain talked with Abel his brother; and it came to pass, when they were in the field, that Cain rose up against Abel his brother and killed him. Then the Lord said to Cain, "Where is Abel your brother?" He said, "I do not know. Am I my brother's keeper?" And He said, "What have you done? The voice of your brother's blood cries out to Me from the ground. So now you are cursed from the earth, which has opened its mouth to receive your brother's blood from your hand. When you till the ground, it shall no longer yield its strength to you. A fugitive and a vagabond you shall be on the earth."

The word *blood* in verse 10 is interesting in that in the Hebrew it is plural. This implies it is not just speaking of Abel, but of those descendants who will now not have their destinies fulfilled in the earth. Abel's blood is crying out for justice, not just for Abel, but for all the progeny of Abel who were denied their destinies in the earth.

The shedding of innocent blood carries a serious legal penalty in the realm of the spirit. Covenants made by blood that unites the parties together for any reason or purpose are a legal union of a vastly serious nature in the realm of the spirit. Blood sacrifices are also extremely powerful instruments that carry spiritually legal results.

At this point I want to introduce two very important points that will help you to understand this legal dimension of the spirit realm that has to be considered to live a successful Christian life. These two points are the meaning of the word *legal* and the importance of another word used by Jesus and Peter in the New Testament that unveil the importance of understanding one of the ways our enemy, the devil, works to hinder our rights and privileges as born-again believers legally. That word is *adversary*.

When defining the word *legal* as it relates to the Courts of Heaven revelation, we are not referring to "legalism" as it relates to religion or the Law of Moses. We are speaking about spiritual laws that have existed from eternity.

Spiritual laws are the highest laws in existence. Spiritual laws have their origin from God Himself and emanate from His nature, character, and integrity. Before there was a physical universe as we know it, when all that existed was the spirit dimension, eternal spiritual laws governed the spirit realm, and they still govern today.

John 4:24 states that God is spirit. He is a spirit being, but He is more than that. He is spirit; the realm of the spirit exists because God exists. Without Him there would be nothing. Everything finds its beginnings in Him. J. W. C. Wand's translation of Colossians 1:17 gives a good description of what I am attempting to explain: *"He existed before everything and everything derives its being from Him."*[6]

In his excellent book *Operating in the Courts of Heaven* Robert Henderson makes this statement, "Everything in the spirit realm is about legalities."[7] Another statement I have heard in the course of learning about the Courts of Heaven that has marked my thinking is, "You can't fake the realm of the spirit out!" Oh, how true that statement is!

So many religious people focus on the Law of Moses as the basis of holiness, but the realm of the spirit is governed by a higher set of laws. The laws that govern the spirit realm are what determine the legal basis by which life is judged, whether it is in Heaven, in the earth, or in any other dimension of God's creation. The Law of Moses just describes for man's benefit the kind of behavior that violates those spiritual laws.

The finished work of redemption establishes the legal basis by which a citizen of God's Kingdom can deal with those legal issues to keep the all-important fellowship with God from being hindered should any one of those spiritual laws be violated. It is the relationship established through faith in

Jesus Christ and God's saving grace that allows the believer to handle any legal issues that can be used by the adversary in an attempt to keep their destiny from being fully lived out and realized.

Let us now look at this word *adversary* as presented by Jesus and Peter that will open our eyes to one of the ways that the devil will attempt to resist our rights and privileges in the Kingdom of God.

As Henderson so beautifully explains, Jesus taught on prayer in three different dimensions.[8] Jesus taught prayer as going to God as Father (Luke 11:1-4); going to God as friend (Luke 11:5-8); and going to God as judge (Luke 18:1-8). It is this third dimension of prayer in which Jesus reveals that there will be times when we must go before the Lord as our Righteous Judge so that we can deal with attempts by our enemy to delay our destinies. Jesus reveals that when this happens, we are having to secure a judgment against an adversary.

This word *adversary* found in Luke 18:3 is the Greek word *antidikos* and means "an opponent in a suit of law."[9] This means that our enemy in this case is not attempting to meet us on a battlefield but is using things that are legal in nature with which to hinder us.

I want you to look at this passage from Luke 18:1-8 and notice the context in which Jesus used this word *adversary*:

> *Then He spoke a parable to them, that men always ought to pray and not lose heart, saying: "There was in a certain city a judge who did not fear God nor regard man. Now there was a widow in that city; and*

she came to him, saying, 'Get justice for me from my adversary.' And he would not for a while; but afterward he said within himself, 'Though I do not fear God nor regard man, yet because this widow troubles me I will avenge her, lest by her continual coming she weary me.'" Then the Lord said, "Hear what the unjust judge said. And shall God not avenge His own elect who cry out day and night to Him, though He bears long with them? I tell you that He will avenge them speedily. Nevertheless, when the Son of Man comes, will He really find faith on the earth?"

This situation, from the context of prayer, is not playing out against an opponent who seeks to engage us in a military conflict using tactics that are effective on a battlefield. No, it is plain to see that this is playing out in a courtroom, before a judge, and it is dealing things that are legal in nature.

Our adversary is attempting to use legal things with which to hinder, delay, or deny us something that we have a right to receive, and the strategy is something that is playing out in the presence of a judge in a courtroom. A confirming witness of this strategy that is used by the devil is found in First Peter 5:8: *"Be sober, be vigilant; because your adversary the devil walks about like a roaring lion, seeking whom he may devour."* Adversary in this verse is the same word *antidikos* and means the same thing, "an opponent in a suit of law."

If the devil has no ability to use legal things against us as an adversary who is presenting a legal argument before a judge, then Jesus and Peter would not have used a word that communicates that this is one of the strategies we must be aware of in our dealings with him. Additionally, the Holy Spirit would not have inspired Jesus or Peter to use such a word that communicates that strategy is possible.

This leads us to what should be obvious questions: What would those legal things be that could be strong enough to present before the Courts of Heaven and legally hinder our rights and privileges? If this is a possible strategy that our enemy implements against us, how is he finding these legal things that hold enough validity before the Courts of Heaven to cause us problems, and how do we defeat him when he does?

Anytime blood is shed, it has spiritual implications. Blood speaks; it has a voice. Therefore, the shedding of blood through murder, abortion, human and child sacrifice, and through using either human or animal blood in the cutting of covenants with demon powers, provides evidence and testimony that can be used by the adversary in the Courts of Heaven. This is true anytime people have used blood as an instrument of worship before an altar or as a means of entering into some kind of agreement, or the basis of a trade, to gain help, assistance, or power from demonic powers. All of these activities are all powerful spiritual evidence of a legal nature that our adversary seeks out in our ancestry. Why is this so powerful? Because it introduces iniquity into our bloodline that must be answered by somebody in the family in a legal way to remove it.

Blood cannot be dismissed; it has a voice and cries out for justice when it is shed unjustly or in a way that establishes a covenant that dishonors God and violates spiritual law. Blood covenants must be annulled by a power higher than the power called upon when the covenant was first cut and established. Blood covenants are not just natural; they are first and foremost spiritual. That is why blood covenants are the most powerful agreement that exists. There is no getting out of it.

Western-minded people have a hard time accepting this powerful truth. We have a generational mind-set that, at this point in its development, looks for a quick fix to everything and has lost virtually all sense of real honor and loyalty. This is the root of many of the problems in marriage today.

Blood sins are iniquitous by their very nature because those sins are committed by self-will and carry a heavy spiritual penalty. Even the accidental shedding of blood is a serious matter and can introduce spiritually legal issues that are not to be ignored or dismissed. Blood speaks!

Hebrews 12:22-24 reveals the realm into which we have been raised through union with Christ and where we are to deal with every legal issue that the adversary may attempt to come against us.

> *But you have come to Mount Zion and to the city of the living God, the heavenly Jerusalem, to an innumerable company of angels, to the general assembly and church of the firstborn who are registered in heaven, to God the Judge of all, to the spirits of just men made perfect, to Jesus the Mediator of the new covenant, and to the blood of sprinkling that speaks better things than that of Abel.*

Notice three key phrases in this passage: *"But you have come to Mount Zion."* We have already come to Mount Zion. We are seated in heavenly places with Christ (see Eph. 2:6; Col. 3:1-2). We are not trying to get to Heaven or waiting to go to Heaven if we are born again! We have made it! We are citizens of Heaven right now (see Phil. 3:20).

We have come *"to God the Judge of all."* God, the Righteous Judge, is functioning in His judgeship on our behalf right now, and we stand before Him right now if we are born again. God the Father has actually turned all judgment over to Jesus (see John 5:22), so our blood brother by covenant is our judge, and He is for us and not against us!

We have come *"to the blood of sprinkling that speaks better things than that of Abel."* The blood of Abel cried out for vengeance, but the blood of Jesus cries out for mercy! The testimony of the blood of Jesus is judicial in nature and is speaking things that are legal in nature. The first function of the blood of Jesus on behalf of the born-again believer is to offer testimony that speaks for us in the Court of Heaven. By faith, when we step into the Court of Heaven to agree with that testimony and ask for the blood to silence the accusations and overrule the cases of the adversary, it does its work as a matter of a legal action. This is why the believer has been brought into that realm, to align our words with the words of the blood.

The blood of Jesus is still giving testimony in the Courts of Heaven. Notice what it says in Revelation 12:10-11.

> *Then I heard a loud voice saying in heaven, "Now salvation, and strength, and the kingdom of our God,*

and the power of His Christ have come, for the accuser of our brethren, who accused them before our God day and night, has been cast down. And they overcame him by the blood of the Lamb and by the word of their testimony, and they did not love their lives to the death."

Overcoming the accuser is accomplished by the right testimony being given in the Court of Heaven. As we saw in Hebrews 12:24, the blood speaks in that heavenly dimension we have identified as the Court of Heaven. To speak in a courtroom is to give testimony. The blood of Jesus testifies to everything that Jesus accomplished through the finished work of redemption.

The other requirement is our testimony. Our words need to agree with the testimony of the blood. We need to go into the spirit dimension of the Court of Heaven knowing what the blood of Jesus has accomplished legally for us and offer our testimony, which agrees with the testimony of the blood. Our testimony satisfies the demand for two or three witnesses to give testimony. Deuteronomy 19:15 affirms this truth: *"One witness shall not rise against a man concerning any iniquity or any sin that he commits; by the mouth of two or three witnesses the matter shall be established."*

God's blood is the most powerful matter ever introduced into the universe! However, its efficacy is not automatic when legal cases have been brought before the court by the adversary. We must learn to live out of Heaven now and take advantage of our covenant rights as heavenly priests of the order of Melchizedek on purpose and by faith.

Learning to deal with blood matters from the legal side of the ledger opens up a realm of release and freedom from the adversarial ability of the enemy that is almost indescribable! We can function in Heaven now and work with Jesus to see His purposes accomplished in our lives and in this world.

By the end of this book we will look at the legal strategies to annul the legal agreements based on blood that may still be in your ancestry background that the adversary is using to deny you your right to walk in the benefits of your spiritual inheritance in Christ. We will also get to glimpse into the right and responsibility of the Body of Christ to function from a legal position, from the Courts of Heaven, to free nations from the generational iniquities that are allowing the devil to maintain a legal right to enforce darkness and the curse upon them.

Chapter 4

THE LEGALITY OF WORDS

You don't have to read the Bible all that much to begin to understand that God places a high priority on words. The reason He does this is because He created words to accomplish a specific purpose. Proverbs 18:21 reveals this purpose and the power connected to it: *"Death and life are in the power of the tongue, and those who love it will eat its fruit."*

Words were not originally created by God for the purpose of communication. As purposed and designed by God, words were created for releasing spiritual power; communication is nothing more than a result of fulfilling that purpose.

Jesus indicated that words carry a legal dimension due to the created purpose which they possess. Look at Matthew 12:34-37:

*Brood of vipers! How can you, being evil, speak good
things? For out of the abundance of the heart the
mouth speaks. A good man out of the good treasure of
his heart brings forth good things, and an evil man
out of the evil treasure brings forth evil things. But
I say to you that for every idle word men may speak,
they will give account of it in the day of judgment.
For by your words you will be justified, and by your
words you will be condemned.*

Notice the statement, *"out of the abundance of the heart the
mouth speaks."* Your mouth is connected to your heart, not just
your brain. Your heart is the clearinghouse for everything that
comes into your life and flows out of your influence. What
you say reflects not only the condition of your heart, but it also
releases the predominate spiritual force that is working in your
life. If it isn't in you, it will not come out of you!

This is why what Jesus said in the next verse is so important. *"A good man out of the good treasure of his heart brings forth
good things, and an evil man out of the evil treasure brings forth
evil things."* The word *treasure* can also be translated "deposit."
Let's read it with that meaning: *A good man out of the good
deposit of his heart brings forth good things, and an evil man out of
the evil deposit brings forth evil things.* You can see here that your
words will release the power that is stored up in your heart.

You can also speak words that are essentially worthless
with respect to releasing spiritual power. *"But I say to you that
for every idle word men may speak, they will give account of it in
the day of judgment."* Read this verse from the Amplified Bible,

Classic Edition: *"But I tell you, on the day of judgment men will have to give account for every idle (inoperative, nonworking) word they speak."*

Again, I want to reinforce this point. Based upon a careful examination of the Bible, the primary purpose of words is to release spiritual power! This is why Jesus said this vastly important statement in verse 37: *"For by your words you will be justified, and by your words you will be condemned."* Let's look at that from the Amplified Bible: *"For by your words you will be justified and acquitted, and by your words you will be condemned and sentenced"* (AMPC)

The words *justified* and *condemned* are legal words right out of the courtroom, and the fact that the Amplified Bible expands it to include *acquitted* and *sentenced* is in perfect agreement with the Greek language in the original texts. This is hugely important for our understanding!

Words are powerful, and words are legal. In other words, the adversary is listening to our words to develop a case based upon the testimony of our own mouths! He is literally listening to every word you speak, and he will use them against you in a legal manner if the words release power in a way that violates spiritual law.

Words are spiritual because you, as a spirit being, have a free will with which to choose the words you speak, which in turn release spiritual power. We know that is true in that we can greatly influence people with the words we speak to them or around them. But we also know that is true from the revelation of the Word of God.

Notice what Jesus said in John 6:63: *"It is the Spirit who gives life; the flesh profits nothing. The words that I speak to you are spirit, and they are life."* Notice, Jesus said the words He speaks are spirit and life. Thus we come to understand spoken words are spiritual in nature, and words have the capacity to be life itself! The words are life. They don't just communicate life, they are life!

That is in perfect agreement with Proverbs 18:21. Life words acquit us; death words sentence us. That is what I mean by words are legal. So, we have to understand that if we have been using words improperly, there is a great potential that the adversary has been able to build a case against us to legally enforce the curse against us based on our words alone.

As I brought up in the previous chapter, Deuteronomy 19:15 is a courtroom verse that dictates where testimony is concerned. *"One witness shall not rise against a man concerning any iniquity or any sin that he commits; by the mouth of two or three witnesses the matter shall be established."* If our words give testimony that the accuser can use against us to his advantage, don't think for a moment he will not attempt to do that. Our words need to agree with the blood!

Remember, in chapter 2 we established that iniquity at its root is self-will. Because we choose the words we speak, we are using our will to release testimony in the realm of the spirit on a continual basis. Iniquitous words are words that we chose to speak that give our adversary an advantage over us. It is those words that he will use against us to legally enforce the curse against us. Proverbs 26:2 is instructive on this matter, *"Like a flitting sparrow, like a flying swallow, so a curse without cause shall not alight."*

The adversary knows that in order to enforce something such as a terminal disease on a Christian, he has to have a strong case to legally resist our efforts to receive healing. It was something legal that allowed that disease to land, and it is something legal that keeps it in place until either we remove the legal issues through the Courts of Heaven, or the enemy successfully runs out the clock and the disease destroys our physical body's ability to sustain our spirit's presence in this planet.

The devil will use illegal means to bring attacks against believers. Life-threatening sicknesses, for the most part, have some kind of doorway into the life of a believer connected to iniquity in some form or fashion. Those types of situations cannot be turned through spiritual warfare alone; they must be addressed in the Courts of Heaven.

The reason we need to understand the legal nature of our words is revealed in how Jesus indicated how He had to avoid using words in a way that would cross the line by self-willed actions and speaking. What He said in Matthew 12, which we just looked at, should give you a sense of the high premium Jesus placed upon the spoken word. It also gives us insight into the legal dimension of words that Jesus Himself had to live His life in the light of every moment of every day.

Every temptation Jesus was faced with was, at its very root, a temptation to take a step of self-will. He could not afford to do anything of His own accord or initiative. He had to be completely and totally committed to only do and only say what He saw and heard from His Father. To do otherwise would have been to commit iniquity.

The idea that Jesus could just walk around and do whatever He wanted to do and say whatever He wanted to say just because He was the Son of God, is a religious idea that does not hold water in the light of what Jesus Himself said concerning how He lived. The following passages from the Gospel of John are very revealing of the tight constraints our Lord had to observe to avoid disqualifying Himself from being able to be the Lamb without spot or blemish.

> *So Jesus said, "I speak to you timeless truth. The Son is not able to do anything from himself or through my own initiative. I only do the works that I see the Father doing, for the Son does the same works as his Father"* (John 5:19 TPT).

> *I can do nothing on My own initiative. As I hear, I judge; and My judgment is just, because I do not seek My own will, but the will of Him who sent Me* (John 5:30 NASB).

> *For I have come down from Heaven, not to do what I want, but to do the will of him who sent me* (John 6:38 PNT).

> *Jesus answered them and said, "My teaching, is not Mine, but His who sent Me"* (John 7:16 NASB).

> *"I have many things to speak and to judge concerning you, but He who sent Me is true; and the things which I heard from Him, these I speak to the world."*

They did not realize that He had been speaking to them about the Father. So Jesus said, "When you lift up the Son of Man, then you will know that I am He, and I do nothing on My own initiative, but I speak these things as the Father taught Me. And He who sent Me is with Me; He has not left Me alone, for I always do the things that are pleasing to Him" (John 8:26-29 NASB).

For I did not speak on My own initiative, but the Father Himself who sent Me has given Me a commandment as to what to say and what to speak. I know that His commandment is eternal life; therefore the things I speak, I speak just as the Father has told Me (John 12:49-50 NASB).

Do you not believe that I am in the Father, and the Father is in Me? The words that I say to you I do not speak on My own initiative, but the Father abiding in Me does His works (John 14:10 NASB).

Notice that Jesus repeated over and over the fact that He said nothing but what He heard from the Father; He was here to only do what the Father wanted done. Self-will was not an option if He was going to fulfill the desires of His Father.

The greatest test of resisting self-will was when He faced the reality of what would happen when He went to the cross. He was not considering the pain and suffering that He would endure physically. He faced the loss of the most precious thing in His earthly existence—the constant and continual fellowship with His Father. He knew that He would have to enter the realm of spiritual death, the source of all the problems of mankind and in the earth, and in obedience to His Father become obedient to this enemy, which had held mankind captive since the fall of Adam.

In the Garden of Gethsemane, Jesus separated Himself from the disciples and agonized in prayer. Luke records this in chapter 22, verses 41-44:

> *And he was withdrawn from them about a stone's cast, and kneeled down, and prayed, Saying, Father, if thou be willing, remove this cup from me: nevertheless not my will, but thine, be done. And there appeared an angel unto him from heaven, strengthening him. And being in an agony he prayed more earnestly: and his sweat was as it were great drops of blood falling down to the ground* (KJV).

Hebrews 12:4 shows us what He was dealing with and applies it to us. *"After all, you have not yet reached the point of sweating blood in your opposition to sin"* (TPT). He was resisting sin. What sin? The sin of preserving His relationship and fellowship with the Father at the expense of all mankind's future. Satan used the most valuable and precious thing Jesus possessed to tempt Him to the point of sweating great drops of blood! He overcame the greatest test with the words *"nevertheless not My will, but Yours be done"* (Luke 22:42).

He did not commit iniquity so that we could go free from it! This is the great truth behind the finished work of redemption! This is not automatic as far as our complete freedom pertaining to our flesh walk in the earth. In our next chapter we will investigate the New Testament to understand how to deal with things that pertain to our earthly walk and enjoying the physical side of our inheritance in Christ.

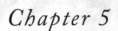

Chapter 5

WHAT IS BLOODLINE INIQUITY?

As we learned earlier, Adam, according to Romans 5:12, threw the entire human race into the prison house of spiritual death by committing iniquity in the Garden of Eden. The infection of sin began to be passed from one generation to another, and at the same time, began to develop an ever-increasing manifestation of incipient death in men's lives.

Bloodline iniquity began to show up in the form of generational behavior and generational mind-sets that were developing under the relentless pressure of satanic influence and temptation. With very little to restrain the influences from the inside out, mankind gradually began to yield in greater measures to the demonic forces that had been unleashed as a result of Adam's failure to take dominion.

As we go back to Romans 5, let's look again at *The Passion Translation* of verses 12-14.

> *When Adam sinned, the entire world was affected. Sin entered human experience, and death was the result. And so death followed this sin, casting its shadow over all humanity, because all have sinned. Sin was in the world before Moses gave the written law, but it was not charged against them where no law existed. Yet death reigned as king from Adam to Moses even though they hadn't broken a command the way Adam had. The first man, Adam, was a picture of the Messiah, who was to come.*

It is important to understand that God could not hold men accountable for their sin between Adam and Moses because there was no law given to define sin and by which men could be judged. Even though men were not having their sin imputed against them by God, the spiritual law of sin and death was still doing its deadly work. Once God introduced the Law through Moses, men could be justly judged because they now had knowledge of sin.

Iniquity in the bloodline was a judgment that could extend to the third and fourth generations of a family. Pay particular attention to the way God describes Himself to Moses in Exodus 34:6-7.

> *And the Lord passed before him and proclaimed, "The Lord, the Lord God, merciful and gracious, longsuffering, and abounding in goodness and truth, keeping*

mercy for thousands, **forgiving iniquity and trans-gression and sin,** *by no means clearing the guilty,* **visiting the iniquity of the fathers upon the children and the children's children to the third and the fourth generation.**"

Notice God said that He forgives iniquity, transgression, and sin. So, we need to understand that these are three separate things. They are not the same in the way that God looks at them or deals with them. The best way to break this down is to look at the way Jesus showed the differences.

Jesus taught the principles that would govern the new covenant of grace; He did not teach the Law. He came to fulfill the Law of Moses, and by so doing, with His shed blood, instituted a new covenant where the only way to get into that covenant is to be re-fathered from above. The new birth is the only way to enter into covenant with God in this age of grace.

He was constantly contrasting the principles of the Law of Moses with the principles of grace. The reason for this was to lay the groundwork of the way a truly born-again believer would live, which was a lifestyle of being led from the inside by the Holy Spirit as opposed to being led from the outside by a written code. The author of the Law of Moses was going to take up residence in the heart of men as a result of receiving the grace gift of righteousness through the new birth. Therefore, the means to deal with disobedience when it begins as a thought would replace the outside-in lifestyle under the Law of Moses, which only dealt with sin and transgression after the act was performed.

Notice this contrast in the following passage from the Book of Matthew.

> *You have heard that it was said to those of old, "You shall not murder, and whoever murders will be in danger of the judgment." But I say to you that whoever is angry with his brother without a cause shall be in danger of the judgment. And whoever says to his brother, "Raca!" shall be in danger of the council. But whoever says, "You fool!" shall be in danger of hell fire. Therefore if you bring your gift to the altar, and there remember that your brother has something against you, leave your gift there before the altar, and go your way. First be reconciled to your brother, and then come and offer your gift. Agree with your adversary quickly, while you are on the way with him, lest your adversary deliver you to the judge, the judge hand you over to the officer, and you be thrown into prison. Assuredly, I say to you, you will by no means get out of there till you have paid the last penny. You have heard that it was said to those of old, "You shall not commit adultery." But I say to you that whoever looks at a woman to lust for her has already committed adultery with her in his heart. If your right eye causes you to sin, pluck it out and cast it from you; for it is more profitable for you that one of your members perish, than for your whole body to be cast into hell. And if your right hand causes you to sin, cut it off and cast it from you; for it is more profitable for you that*

one of your members perish, than for your whole body to be cast into hell (Matthew 5:21-30).

This passage is loaded with revelation that opens our eyes to the importance of understanding the legal dimension of the realm of the spirit. The shift from the Law of Moses to the gift of grace did not change the legal dimension of the spirit realm; nor did it change the way the adversary seeks to use legal things against God's people. It did open the door for the believer to be able to answer those legal challenges on the basis of what Jesus accomplished in His death, burial, resurrection, and ascension. Because of the new birth, the believer has the ability to stop sin when it is still in the form of a seed, as a thought. Grace empowers us to be able to stop things before they manifest in the open.

Let's consider this part of what Jesus said:

Therefore if you bring your gift to the altar, and there remember that your brother has something against you, leave your gift there before the altar, and go your way. First be reconciled to your brother, and then come and offer your gift. Agree with your adversary quickly, while you are on the way with him, lest your adversary deliver you to the judge, the judge hand you over to the officer, and you be thrown into prison. Assuredly, I say to you, you will by no means get out of there till you have paid the last penny (vv. 23-26).

This is dealing with personal relationships. Disagreements, strife, anger, and other emotional relational matters are the seedbed of a massive amount of thoughts and behaviors that can escalate to the point that destinies can be severely altered and even destroyed. These instructions have to do with relationships within the Body of Christ, between believers.

There are many things that can cause your giving to produce the wrong testimony in the realm of the spirit. Strife is a major issue that can cause your giving to not produce the desired harvest. Jesus is teaching that when there is strife between you and another believer, it is important to get things reconciled before you offer your gift. The reason is not because God is upset with you; it's because your adversary (same Greek word, *antidikos*) can use the situation to initiate a legal case against you.

Remember, you cannot fake the realm of the spirit out. It is better to acknowledge that things aren't right between you and another believer and get it straightened out, than to try and act like everything is alright when it is not. The longer you let things drift without dealing with them, the longer the adversary has to pursue a case against you and legally deny you your harvest, delay promotions, or frustrate the purposes and destiny that God has planned for you. You will not stop the damage until you repent and make things right. It can boil down to the question of how much pain can you endure before you do the right thing and get things reconciled.

The problem that God has in these situations is that He cannot pervert justice, even when the devil has brought the case against you. If it is true that there is strife there, God cannot move on your behalf when the adversary brings it up as a legal case. I am always reminded when talking about the dangers of strife of what the apostle Paul wrote to Timothy on this subject. The King James Version still carries so much weight in this passage.

> *But foolish and unlearned questions avoid, knowing that they do gender strifes. And the servant of the Lord must not strive; but be gentle unto all men, apt to teach, patient, in meekness instructing those that oppose themselves; if God peradventure will give them repentance to the acknowledging of the truth; and that they may recover themselves out of the snare of the devil, who are taken captive by him at his will* (2 Timothy 2:23-26).

Strife is deadly! When you are in strife, you can be taken captive at satan's will! He will move in on that situation and bring a lawsuit before the Court of Heaven against all the believers who are in that fuss and use that legal case as a way to delay, deny, or destroy the destinies of everyone involved. Even after the fuss is over, if the case is not dealt with and the accusations silenced by repentance and forgiveness, the adversary will keep that case in place to frustrate the will of God in the lives of those who were involved.

Then Jesus describes the level at which sin takes place under grace in this next section.

> *You have heard that it was said to those of old, "You shall not commit adultery." But I say to you that whoever looks at a woman to lust for her has already*

committed adultery with her in his heart (Matthew 5:27-28).

Under the Law of Moses, you were not guilty of adultery until you actually committed the act. Jesus is introducing a much tougher standard, the standard that applies under grace. Under grace you become guilty when you lust in your heart and have the desire to have sexual relations with someone, even if you never act it out. Why? Because under grace you can stop things when they are still in seed form, in the heart and mind and as thoughts. This was not possible under the Law of Moses.

If you meditate and see yourself doing it with the intention of carrying it out if given the opportunity, you are guilty of it. This is the time to judge it and stop it, so that it goes no further. You are to judge yourself of the intention before it becomes a transgression. Grace teaches you to deal with it before it happen (see Titus 2:11-12). It also enables you to have the Holy Spirit deal with you in your heart, and this keeps things from getting complicated and messy as well.

The next part of Jesus's teaching is critical to understand as well. It gives us a glimpse into the nature of bloodline iniquity.

> *If your right eye causes you to sin, pluck it out and cast it from you; for it is more profitable for you that one of your members perish, than for your whole body to be cast into hell. And if your right hand causes you to sin, cut it off and cast it from you; for it is more profitable*

for you that one of your members perish, than for your whole body to be cast into hell (vv. 29-30).

Jesus is not saying you should actually cut off offending members of your physical body. He is instructing us to deal with those things that cause us to sin. We can be dealing with bloodline patterns of behavior that we can see the pattern in our family's history. The right eye and right hand are indicating things that have a certain amount of authority in our lives and affect our physical passions. This is bloodline iniquity and needs to be explained so that we can understand how it influences our lives.

Remember this phrase I highlighted from Exodus 34:7: *"visiting the iniquity of the fathers upon the children and the children's children to the third and the fourth generation."* Here is what God is communicating here. When sin becomes a generational pattern, it is an indication that what may have started out as just a one-time sin or transgression has now become iniquitous in nature. It now is being passed down through the bloodline and has become a legal issue of serious consequences.

We are not responsible for the sins of our fathers. However, generational behavior is an indication that behavioral patterns and mind-sets have taken hold at the level of our DNA and genes so that a propensity for certain behaviors is being passed down in our bloodlines. This iniquitous inheritance is directly connected to the infection introduced by Adam as head of the human race and, quite frankly, has been developing since he sinned in the Garden of Eden.

Just take a moment and consider the behavioral patterns you see in your own family. What are the common behavioral characteristics you see in your grandparents (even great-grandparents), parents, siblings, and even in your own children? You can even see it in your grandchildren many times. Mind-sets and behaviors that are common and passed from one generation to another are indications of bloodline inheritance.

There is a wealth of material even from the realm of science that indicates that our genetic codes can carry predisposed markers that given the right signals will energize certain genes that produce certain generational patterns. The keys to what will energize the genetic codes are based upon many factors, far beyond the scope or focus of this book. But having a predisposition for something does not necessarily lock you into manifesting a behavior that is the result of inherited iniquity.

Two verses of Scripture are key to understanding a basic biblical explanation for what triggers many behaviors that are inherited. Proverbs 18:21 and Proverbs 23:7 deal with the two main triggers: thoughts and words. Take these two elements and understand that these can be inherited from our bloodline culture. First Peter 1:18-19 speaks to this clearly:

> *Knowing that you were not redeemed with corruptible things, like silver or gold, from your aimless conduct received by tradition from your fathers, but with the precious blood of Christ, as of a lamb without blemish and without spot.*

Dr. William Barclay, who was an internationally recognized Greek scholar, renders these verses in a clear and concise manner in his excellent translation of the New Testament.

> For you know well what it cost to liberate you from the slavery of that life of futility which you inherited from your fathers. The price did not consist of things which are doomed to decay, of silver and gold. The price was the precious life-blood of Christ, who was, as it were, the sacrificial lamb with no flaw or blemish.[10]

We are responsible for our own thinking and behavior, even when that thinking and behavior are a result of a mindset or behavior we inherited generationally. It may not be your fault that you are yielding to things even on an unconscious level, but you are responsible to do something to change it and stop it.

In her excellent book *Switch on Your Brain*, Dr. Caroline Leaf shares this important insight. "The sins of parents create a *predisposition*, not a *destiny*. You are not responsible for something you are predisposed to because of ancestral decisions. You are responsible, however, to be aware of the predispositions, evaluate them, and choose to eliminate them."[11]

You might be thinking at this point, why didn't my salvation free me from all of this? My answer would be you were, but it is not automatic. An important key to learning about how to walk in the full benefits of the finished work of redemption is to understand what was automatic and what wasn't when you got born again. Not understanding this has been the cause of much frustration, misunderstanding, and false judgment by people judging behavior unjustly by not knowing what was going on in the heart of the person they were judging.

Let's work from the inside out as we explain what happens the day you gave your life to Jesus. I will use my own testimony as an example.

I was born again on February 13, 1977, at 3:00 p.m. in the back bedroom of my parent's house where I lived at the time. I was twenty-two years old and had recently returned home after living a life of hard sin and rebellion to both God and my parents. I was unemployed, tired, worn out, and desperate for change in my life. I was a borderline alcoholic, smoked up to three packs of cigarettes a day, and cussed at a high level of expertise. I had become good at yielding to the passions of the flesh and demonic impulses.

When I prayed and asked Jesus into my life, immediately my spirit was born again. According to Second Corinthians 5:17 I became a new creation in Christ. The man that was, at his very core, a hard-core sinner, moved out of spiritual death and was joined by the Holy Spirit in a miraculous work of God's power to become one spirit with the Lord (see 1 Cor. 6:17). My spirit had been recreated, and re-fathered from above (see John 3:3). I was translated out of the authority of darkness and into the Kingdom of God (see Col. 1:13). I was made to sit with Christ at the right hand of the Father in heavenly places and became a citizen of Heaven (see Eph. 2:6; Phil. 3:20). All of this happened in the twinkling of an eye, and my spirit changed from darkness to light, from death to life, and from hate to love. (See the entire book of First John!)

All that was necessary for that to happen was acting on Romans 10:9: *"If you confess with your mouth the Lord Jesus and believe in your heart that God has raised Him from the dead, you will be saved."* I did, and I was. To be saved means to be born again.

Now I had a job to do. I had to renew my mind. Romans 12:1-2 speaks of the two most important things you must do after you get saved.

> *I beseech you therefore, brethren, by the mercies of God, that you present your bodies a living sacrifice, holy, acceptable to God, which is your reasonable service. And do not be conformed to this world, but be transformed by the renewing of your mind, that you may prove what is that good and acceptable and perfect will of God.*

God accepts your body as a holy and acceptable act of worship before Him when you offer it. This has legal implications because when you do that, He is now responsible to help you cleanse and purge it so that it will not be a constant source of trouble to your walk of faith. I will deal with this later.

The second thing that we need to do is to renew our minds. We come into the Kingdom of God with mind-sets that have been shaped and programmed by the culture of our family; by the culture of the city, state, region, and nation where we were born and grew up; by the religious orientation we were raised within; and many other influences that we did not have much control over and sometimes were forced upon us. Very little of this programming prepares us to walk in agreement with the culture of the Kingdom of God or to be able to cooperate with the Spirit of God to any great degree.

Add to this the generational mind-sets that we inherited and influence our thinking on such a deep level that it literally is an unconscious influence that shapes the way we respond and react to the kaleidoscope situations and circumstances we deal with on a day-to-day basis. Very little of this preprogramming we actually chose for ourselves. So, we must begin to, on purpose, work to change the entire body of thinking that we already have to come in ever-increasing alignment with the mind of Christ and with Heaven's culture.

Mind renewal is not scripture memorization. It is changing the way you think at a core level. It is an ongoing discipline of replacing mind-sets, beliefs, rules, values, and references to bring your thinking and the thinking processes that govern you at the unconscious level to agree with what will allow you to be more accurately led by the Holy Spirit and think and respond like Jesus thinks and responds. It is, without a doubt, hard work. I will touch on some the keys to accomplish mind renewal later in this book.

I will just add this one statement that you need to understand in the light of what I am addressing right now. Mind renewal is not automatic, and it is your responsibility. God will not renew your mind, and your mind did not get renewed when you got born again. Much more could be said about this, but it's enough to say that this is not an automatic result of salvation.

This leads me to say that on February 13, 1977, when I got born again, I sensed that things were different, and that awareness energized me with a great amount of excitement. I was alive spiritually, and it had a positive effect on my outlook on life and my attitude. But as I was to discover in the days and weeks ahead, old thinking and behavioral patterns were still there, and as a result, a lot of my behavior did not reflect the change in my spirit.

My spirit didn't have a whole lot to work with in my soul, which is made up of my mind, my emotions, and my will. My mind, made up of the subconscious mind where all the renewing needed to take place, was still programmed according to thinking, speaking, and behaving that developed under satanic influences for the most part, especially over the previous seven to eight years. Now I had to get to work and put into my mind things that agreed with the new creation I had become. After over forty years of mind renewal, I am a whole lot further down the road now, but I still have so much work to do!

What about my physical body? Well, according to Romans 8:23, my body didn't get born again either! *"Not only that, but we also who have the firstfruits of the Spirit, even we ourselves groan within ourselves, eagerly waiting for the adoption, the redemption of our body."*

My body is not redeemed yet! My spirit is redeemed; my mind is having to have redemption programmed into it on an ever-increasing basis; and I have to enforce redemption upon this physical body. Healing from sickness and disease is not automatic! I have to learn how to take authority over my body and exercise dominion over it.

On the day I got born again, the physical passions, desires, and appetites of my physical body were all aligned with everything that was, if not illegal, certainly immoral, not conducive to living to the highest degree of health.

I would soon discover that the desires that fueled my fleshly appetites had an iniquitous root that had been developed over many generations in my family bloodlines and made certain desires and behaviors have an addictive nature about them. The harder I tried to change, the more challenging it became to subdue those behaviors and the thinking and emotions connected to them. Some of these things I was unable to conquer until I discovered the power of the Courts of Heaven and found out how to cleanse the iniquities that gave the adversary a legal right to keep the pressure on my flesh and my mind. After a forty-year battle with those things, I am completely free, and the temptations are totally gone!

The subduing of my physical body and enforcing redemption upon it was not automatic. I found out that due to Adam's inheritance in the flesh and the development of generational iniquity as inherited from my family bloodlines, I had to learn how to free my physical body from the grip of things that were afflicting me even as a result of my DNA and genetic predispositions. Tough discipline had only gone so far in bringing results, and even after years of riding herd on my flesh, I would find that the pressure of temptation would get so strong that I would yield just to get the pressure off. This was unacceptable, but until I found out what I could do to get rid of the source of the temptation in the Courts of Heaven, it was the way things were.

In the next chapter I will show you the revelation from the New Testament that describes what I learned and has enabled me to conquer things in my life that had plagued me for all my born-again experience, going back to that wonderful day in February 1977. There truly is *victory* in Jesus!

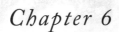

Chapter 6

BECOMING A VESSEL
OF HONOR

As we learned in the previous chapter, Jesus' sacrifice at Calvary and the finished work of redemption that was the result of His sacrifice opened the door to spiritual union with God through the new birth. Anyone on this planet can get born again by receiving Jesus as Lord.

The born-again believer is a new creature (some translators use the term "new species"). The Holy Spirit recreates the human spirit and brings the believer into a spiritual union of complete oneness with the Lord Jesus. God accomplishes this miracle as a marvelous work of His power and grace. God's grace accomplished what we could never have accomplished on our own.

As stated earlier, the mind is not born again, so we must renew our mind to the Word of God and the culture of the

Kingdom of God by meditating on God's Word and install-ing, as it were, a new program which allows the mind of Christ to begin to have an ever-increasing influence on our thinking and behavior.

This mind renewal project and the job of subduing the passions and desires of our physical body offer plenty of oppor-tunities to experience roadblocks to our spiritual progress. The full benefits of being in union with the Lord through the power and presence of the Holy Spirit as well as our spiritual seating with Christ in Heaven afford us the necessary tools to accomplish the job.

We don't realize just how far our thinking, speaking, and motivations are out of sync with the way the Holy Spirit needs us cooperating with Him in these areas in our lives to align with the purposes and plans of God when we begin our spir-itual journey with Christ. There are two passages that give a description of our training and condition before we were born again.

> *And you He made alive, who were dead in tres-passes and sins, in which you once walked according to the course of this world, according to the prince of the power of the air, the spirit who now works in the sons of disobedience, among whom also we all once conducted ourselves in the lusts of our flesh, ful-filling the desires of the flesh and of the mind, and were by nature children of wrath, just as the others* (Ephesians 2:1-3).

This I say, therefore, and testify in the Lord, that you should no longer walk as the rest of the Gentiles walk, in the futility of their mind, having their understanding darkened, being alienated from the life of God, because of the ignorance that is in them, because of the blindness of their heart; who, being past feeling, have given themselves over to lewdness, to work all uncleanness with greediness (Ephesians 4:17-19).

This is the condition we come into the Kingdom of God having experienced prior to the new birth. The number of years you lived before you got born again is the number of years you developed in darkness. The new birth changed your spirit, but your mind and body were not. Add to this the fact that you have ways of thinking, prejudices, biases, inclinations, and predispositions that are inherited and operating on a subconscious level, and you can see why you struggle at times to live in victory after you are born again.

As we have already established, Romans 8:23 reveals our bodies are not redeemed yet. That leaves our bodies in a state that is at odds with our recreated spirits. We have to master the body and bring it into subjection to our spirit. The apostle Paul speaks about this in First Corinthians 9:24-27.

Do you not know that those who run in a race all run, but one receives the prize? Run in such a way that you may obtain it. And everyone who competes for the prize is temperate in all things. Now they do it to obtain a perishable crown, but we for an imperishable crown. Therefore I run thus: not with uncertainty.

*Thus I fight: not as one who beats the air. **But I discipline my body and bring it into subjection,** lest, when I have preached to others, I myself should become disqualified.*

The weak link in our makeup, is the physical body. We must take charge of it and rule over it, or it will rule over us and keep us vulnerable and subject to being defeated. The physical body is described in these terms in First Corinthians 15:42-50.

*The body is sown in **corruption,** it is raised in incorruption. It is sown in **dishonor,** it is raised in glory. It is sown in **weakness,** it is raised in power. It is sown a **natural** body, it is raised a spiritual body. There is a natural body, and there is a spiritual body. And so it is written, "The first man Adam became a living being." The last Adam became a life-giving spirit. However, the spiritual is not first, but the natural, and afterward the spiritual. The first man was of the earth, made of dust; the second Man is the Lord from heaven. As was the man of dust, so also are those who are made of dust; and as is the heavenly Man, so also are those who are heavenly. And as we have borne the image of the man of dust, we shall also bear the image of the heavenly Man. Now this I say, brethren, that flesh and blood cannot inherit the kingdom of God; nor does corruption inherit incorruption.*

Notice the words *corruption, dishonor, weakness,* and *natural.* These all describe the condition of our physical body as it relates to the new creation spirit. Our spirit is a new creation, designed by God to function and inherit everything that Jesus accomplished for us in the finished work of redemption right now. Our physical body cannot inherit the Kingdom of God due to its present condition. It has to be subdued from within, but our new creation spirits have already inherited the Kingdom of God through union with Christ Jesus.

Our physical body is the one aspect of our makeup that has to be brought into submission, and it is our responsibility to do so. There is a very powerful bit of instruction that the apostle Paul gave in First Thessalonians 4:3-8 that is pertinent to what we are learning at this point.

> *For this is the will of God, your sanctification: that you should abstain from sexual immorality; **that each of you should know how to possess his own vessel in sanctification and honor**, not in passion of lust, like the Gentiles who do not know God; that no one should take advantage of and defraud his brother in this matter, because the Lord is the avenger of all such, as we also forewarned you and testified. For God did not call us to uncleanness, but in holiness. Therefore he who rejects this does not reject man, but God, who has also given us His Holy Spirit.*

Repeatedly, we see that the New Testament emphasizes the need for our sanctification and the need to perfect holiness in our lives. There is a reason this is so. In Second Corinthians 3 and 4, the apostle Paul explains how the glory of the old covenant and Mosaic Law is far exceeded by the glory of the new covenant.

He also explains how that the glory of the new covenant is the light of the knowledge of the glory of God in the face of Jesus Christ, and that light is shining in the hearts of those who have been born again. He describes it this way in Second Corinthians 4:7: *"But we have this treasure in earthen vessels, that the excellence of the power may be of God and not of us."*

Notice, that glory is already in us; it is contained within our physical bodies that are called earthen vessels. It is these earthen vessels that must be dealt with if we are to ever give a full and proper expression of that glory. We have to learn how to take dominion over the part of the earth we are wearing and bring it into submission to our spirits.

Our spirits have been glorified through union with Christ. Our physical bodies will be glorified when our blood is changed into the glory that is already the substance of our spirits. It is important that we take a short side journey here to see the role of blood as God designed it to play in our physical bodies.

God gave specific instructions to the children of Israel concerning blood.

> *And whatever man of the house of Israel, or of the strangers who dwell among you, who eats any blood, I will set My face against that person who eats blood, and will cut him off from among his people. **For the life of the flesh is in the blood**, and I have given it to you upon the altar to make atonement for your souls; for it is the blood that makes atonement for the*

soul. Therefore I said to the children of Israel, "No one among you shall eat blood, nor shall any stranger who dwells among you eat blood."

*Whatever man of the children of Israel, or of the strangers who dwell among you, who hunts and catches any animal or bird that may be eaten, he shall pour out its blood and cover it with dust; **for it is the life of all flesh. Its blood sustains its life.** Therefore I said to the children of Israel, "You shall not eat the blood of any flesh, for the life of all flesh is its blood. Whoever eats it shall be cut off"* (Leviticus 17:10-14).

Notice the two highlighted phrases: "*for the life of the flesh is in the blood*" and "*for it is the life of all flesh. Its blood sustains its life.*" The physical body cannot sustain life without the blood. The blood is what sustains the physical body's life.

As I was meditating on this years ago, the Lord asked me a question, "What is the life of the blood?" I had never thought along those lines before. He answered His own question this way, "The life of the blood is the spirit of man." That all of a sudden made perfect sense to me as I thought about it.

Imagine, if you will, the body of Adam in the Garden of Eden just moments after God made it from the ground and just before He breathed life into it. That body was perfect! It had all the parts, in perfection, and had a full supply of blood. It wasn't alive, and it wasn't dead; it was uninhabited. It was the earth suit for the man to wear in the earth that gave him, as a spirit being, the ability to give expression of his being in the earth and have contact with the physical environment as well as live in that environment.

Genesis 2:7 *"And the Lord God formed man of the dust of the ground, and breathed into his nostrils the breath of life; and man became a living being."* Did God blow into the nose of that body? No! He is making a man, not a balloon! God imparted into that physical body the very substance of His own being! And He did this by speaking words. What words?

> *Then God said, "Let Us make man in Our image, according to Our likeness; let them have dominion over the fish of the sea, over the birds of the air, and over the cattle, over all the earth and over every creeping thing that creeps on the earth."*

Those words! Recorded in Genesis 1:26. God used Himself as the pattern for man's body and then spoke to it, standing right in front of it. As He did, His breath entered into that physical body, and spirit life energized the blood in that body. The blood, through the process of transmutation, took the energy of the man's spirit within that body and energized every cell by his presence in the body.

Transmutation is defined as "the change of any thing into another substance, or into something of a different nature."[12] In the way I am applying this word here, the dual nature of blood as God designed it and created it to function, is taking spirit life and energy and changing it into physical life and energy. Blood has both spiritual and physical properties about it, which is why God put restrictions on its use.

Physical death takes place when the spirit of a person leaves that physical body. The blood no longer has the life force of the spirit to transmute to the physical body, or in the case of bleeding out, there is no longer enough blood in the body to perform the task of transmutation to sustain the spirit of a person in their physical body. Blood is truly mystical in the way it functions.

This should make it easy to understand what happened when Adam sinned by committing iniquity. His spirit, the moment he committed the iniquity of eating the fruit, immediately was separated from God as a source of life. His spirit was immediately translated into a state of spiritual death where he now existed as a spirit, cut off from the life of God as its qualitative source.

When that happened, he was also immediately brought under the dominion of satan as his merciless spiritual head and became subject to the darkness and influence of a cursed spiritual state and existence. The blood in his physical body was still carrying the life force of his spirit as physical energy, but rather than that being a creative power that kept every cell in perfection, spiritual death introduced corruption, defilement, and weakness. Adam went from being an eternal man, designed by God to live forever on the earth to becoming a mortal man subject and doomed to death.

As we have already shown from Romans 5:12, the head of the human race introduced an infection of iniquity into the blood that immediately began to degrade the genetic quality of the physical body and ever so gradually began to shorten man's physical life span on this planet. The blood was transmuting a condition of death rather than life, darkness instead of light, hatred instead of love.

It is the unredeemed physical body that carries the iniquitous infection that gives the devil the legal right to keep pressure on the mind with inflamed passions and desires of the flesh until that pressure causes a person to cave into their resistance and sin. It is also the death-infused spirit that has little or no ability to keep ungodly thoughts from taking root, and at best, builds strongholds of fear, unbelief, and pride, which become blinders to the Light of the truth; or at the very worst, through entirely demonized imaginations devises wickedness and evil that is demonstrated through a life in the flesh of an absolute expression of satan's depraved nature.

Going back to what we were discussing before we took this side journey, our physical bodies will have to be changed to experience its redemption. That will happen either through death and resurrection, or being changed before physical death takes place at the coming of the Lord.

The glorification of the body is nothing more than our blood being changed, in the twinkling of an eye, into glory. This supernatural miracle of transmutation of the blood itself into the glory of God will only be possible for those who have already had their spirits glorified through the new creation, which is the re-creation of their spirits through union with Christ. In that moment, you will go from corruption to incorruption, from mortality to immortality, and from being an earthly, natural body to a spiritual body, just like what Jesus had after His resurrection.

Until that takes place, the born-again believer must take dominion over his physical body. This is not something that can be done in our own strength but is done by learning how to take advantage of our spiritual union with Christ, and by the power of the Holy Spirit who lives within us. Learning how to live from the inside out is a major key to success in overcoming the pressures that the five physical senses apply to our minds and using all the spiritual tools and equipment that God has provided for our use.

Cleansing our mind and bodies of the things that the enemy uses to his advantage to get us to yield to his pressure is of such importance that I can hardly find the words to emphasize it. So much of what makes life a challenge for the born-again believer is connected to the already installed mind-sets and the iniquities of our bloodlines that provide legal avenues into our lives for the adversary to exploit to his advantage. It is our job and responsibility to take care of these things. God did what we could not do for ourselves in providing the new birth through union with Christ. We now use our union with Christ and all that affords us to take dominion over this earthy body; cleanse our blood of the iniquitous things we inherited from our ancestors; cleanse our minds of the old mind-sets, much of which was inherited as well; and renew our minds to align with the mind of Christ.

This is a process, and we will never actually get to a place where we have arrived. We can, through diligence, discipline, and determination to please our heavenly Father, work with the Holy Spirit and become progressively more conformed to the image of Jesus Christ and exhibit in the earth an ever-increasing expression of what true sons of God are designed to manifest in this earth. This is the process I call becoming a vessel of honor as described in Second Timothy 2:19-21.

> *Nevertheless the solid foundation of God stands, having this seal: "The Lord knows those who are His," and, "Let everyone who names the name of Christ depart from iniquity." But in a great house there are not only vessels of gold and silver, but also of wood and clay, some for honor and some for dishonor. Therefore if anyone cleanses himself from the latter, he will be a vessel for honor, sanctified and useful for the Master, prepared for every good work.*

Take notice of this statement, *"Let everyone who names the name of Christ depart from iniquity."* This is significant! We are to have nothing to do with iniquity and to essentially sever all ties to it. Keep this in mind as you read the rest of this passage.

> *But in a great house there are not only vessels of gold and silver, but also of wood and clay, some for honor and some for dishonor. Therefore if anyone cleanses himself from the latter, he will be a vessel for honor, sanctified and useful for the Master, prepared for every good work.*

I want to focus on the fact that the cleansing that is mentioned here is a cleansing that we must do, and it is our choice to do it. Jesus is not going to do this for us, and it is not a cleansing that has already taken place. This is something that we must do, and it is changing our "earthen vessel," which is our physical body, into a vessel of gold and silver. This is indicative of bringing our physical body into a state where it is able to function under the anointing of God and give expression—in some degree—to the glory that is already in our spirits. This process of purging actually can determine your usefulness to the Master!

We are not predestined to be dishonorable vessels of wood and clay. God has given us the capacity and ability to be vessels of honor that are like that of gold and silver. It is our choice. And we make that choice by cleansing ourselves. I will reference this again in a bit.

I want you to consider something that is said in First John 3:1-3.

> *Behold what manner of love the Father has bestowed on us, that we should be called children of God! Therefore the world does not know us, because it did not know Him. Beloved, now we are children of God; and it has not yet been revealed what we shall be, but we know that when He is revealed, we shall be like Him, for we shall see Him as He is. And everyone who has this hope in Him purifies himself, just as He is pure.*

Notice this, that we are the children (or sons) of God right now if we are born again. This isn't something we are becoming or will become; we are God's sons and daughters right now, because we are born of Him through union with Christ! This is the new creation which is spoken of in Second Corinthians 5:17-21. As new creation beings we have been made, in our spirits, the very righteousness of God through union with Christ! That is what you are right now as a born-again believer.

But notice verse 3 in First John 3: "*Everyone who has this hope in Him purifies himself, just as He is pure.*" If you are already righteous through union with Christ, then why do you have to purify yourself; and what are you getting rid of when you do that? Our goal in this purification process is to become as pure as Jesus, so we need to identify what this is talking about.

One other passage that speaks along this line is found in Second Corinthians. To get the full scope, we need to read Second Corinthians 6:14-7:1.

> *Do not be unequally yoked together with unbelievers. For what fellowship has righteousness with lawlessness? And what communion has light with darkness? And what accord has Christ with Belial? Or what part has a believer with an unbeliever? And what agreement has the temple of God with idols? For you are the temple of the living God. As God has said: "I will dwell in them and walk among them. I will be their God, and they shall be My people." Therefore "Come out from among them and be separate, says the Lord. Do not touch what is unclean, and I will receive you. I will be a Father to you, and you shall*

*be My sons and daughters, says the Lord Almighty."
Therefore, having these promises, beloved, let us
cleanse ourselves from all filthiness of the flesh and
spirit, perfecting holiness in the fear of God.*

This is an extremely important passage and largely ignored
in our day. I will only touch on some of the instructions here
in order to get to the important point that is made in the first
verse of chapter 7.

*Do not be unequally yoked together with unbelievers.
For what fellowship has righteousness with lawlessness? And what communion has light with darkness?
And what accord has Christ with Belial? Or what
part has a believer with an unbeliever? And what
agreement has the temple of God with idols?*

All of the things listed here are relationships that introduce iniquity into our lives and can become a legal issue that
the adversary can use against us to hinder, delay, or deny our
ability to live out our God-designed destiny. Without going
into detail here, there are things that can completely disrupt
our lives as a result of becoming entangled in these kinds
of relationships.

*For you are the temple of the living God. As God has
said: "I will dwell in them and walk among them.
I will be their God, and they shall be My people."
Therefore "Come out from among them and be separate, says the Lord. Do not touch what is unclean,
and I will receive you. I will be a Father to you, and*

you shall be My sons and daughters, says the Lord Almighty."

This is God's description of our relationship with Him as His sons and daughters. He, God, dwells in us, walks among us, and is our God and we are His people. Because of that reality, He wants us to come out from among those who still are walking in the realm of death and darkness and live lives of separation. Our fellowship, communion, agreement, and covenant commitment are within the context of being in union with Christ. All of these deeply connected relationships are not even possible with those who are still living in a state of spiritual death and walking in the darkness of this world.

We are in the world, but we are not of the world. Jesus prayed this to the Father in John 17. I want to look at verses 14 through 22 for a moment to reinforce some points we are making right now.

> *I have given them Your word; and the world has hated them because they are not of the world, just as I am not of the world. I do not pray that You should take them out of the world, but that You should keep them from the evil one. They are not of the world, just as I am not of the world. Sanctify them by Your truth. Your word is truth. As You sent Me into the world, I also have sent them into the world. And for their sakes I sanctify Myself, that they also may be sanctified by the truth. I do not pray for these alone, but also for those who will believe in Me through their word; that they all may be one, as You, Father, are in Me,*

and I in You; that they also may be one in Us, that the world may believe that You sent Me. And the glory which You gave Me I have given them, that they may be one just as We are one.

Verse 20 is a key verse here. *"I do not pray for these alone, but also for those who will believe in Me through their word."* Jesus brought every born-again believer into this prayer with that statement. Every one of us has experienced the new birth as a result of the words of one or more of the disciples that were with Him the day He prayed that prayer.

That means that everything we read in that prayer has impact on our lives, and we should release our faith and believe we receive the benefits of all that Jesus asked the Father on our behalf. This means that the aspects of protection, sanctification through the Word, being sent by Jesus into the world, and oneness with Jesus and with the Father are all things that we should receive by faith to be operative in our lives too!

This would include what Jesus prayed in verse 22: *"And the glory which You gave Me I have given them, that they may be one just as We are one."* Jesus gave us His glory! That is what we read in Second Corinthians 4:6-7! That glory is in you now and needs to be allowed to shine through you to the world you have been sent into to be a representative of the Kingdom of God and an extension of Jesus Christ's very being and power!

And add to that truth, Jesus also said that the world will hate us, not love us, and you can begin to see that our relationships can be a real help or hindrance to our being able to successfully fulfill our destiny and mission. There is no way to have deeply connected relationships with those whose nature has not changed through union with Christ and it not adversely affect us. Any relationship that we enter into where we are trying to be spiritually connected to an unbeliever is going to have a detrimental effect on our lives personally, and it will hinder our walk with the Lord in ways we may not notice or consider.

We are sent into the world as ambassadors to let the world know of God's love and grace, which has already caused God to reconcile Himself to them. We are not to impute their sins and trespasses against them, but tell them how they need to reconcile themselves to God by receiving Jesus and accepting what He did for them as the way to get connected back to God. Only after they do that can true friendship take place.

Because of all this and the promise that God has made to us with respect to it, we must cleanse ourselves from all defilement that is in our flesh and spirit. Once again, we have to do the cleansing; God will not do it. It is something that has to be done; it is not yet done.

This word *cleanse* is the Greek word *katharizo* and means "to cleanse in a moral sense, to free from defilement of sin."[13] Why would we have to do this? Because our physical bodies are corrupt from their connection to Adam, and our minds have thinking that is defiled from growing up with the influence of the world. God cannot and will not take care of that level of defilement; we must do that. Again we see this in Second Corinthians 7:1: *"Therefore, having these promises, beloved, let us cleanse ourselves from all filthiness of the flesh and spirit, perfecting holiness in the fear of God.*

Perfecting holiness is our responsibility. All three of the words we have seen in the passages from Second Timothy 2, First John 3, and Second Corinthians 7 speak of our responsibility to purge, purify, and cleanse ourselves of anything and everything that would hinder us from walking in an ever-increasing expression of God's power, authority, and glory. This is primarily speaking of the need to keep our earth walk properly managed so that we are not providing legal rights to the adversary to begin building cases against us which can hinder the purposes of God in our lives. We live in a defiled environment in this earth, and if we get lazy with the stewardship of our minds and physical bodies, we can become defiled and not even realize it. It is entirely up to us if we are to become vessels of honor, sanctified and purified so that we are fit for the Master's use!

As I have already mentioned, the way the word is used in relation to the Courts of Heaven has nothing to do with religious legalism. Legalism in that sense is rules and regulations—what you can do and what you shouldn't do; it is performance-based Christianity that is nothing more than an extension of the Law, only using men's laws and what men have determined is right and wrong on some arbitrary determination that they have created. Much of this comes from a misapplication of the Bible, or misinterpretation of even individual verses of the Bible that are purposefully designed to put people in a legalistic form of holiness.

That kind of legalism is not designed to foster intimacy with God and enable you to walk as sons of God in the anointing and power of God. No, it is designed to be a strict standard by which people can be judged and punished. It is an outside-in system of performance-based holiness and righteousness that fosters more bondage than anything else. So, understand that is not what is meant in this book or in the Courts of Heaven understanding of legal things.

I repeat, legal things with respect to the Courts of Heaven, are the things the adversary uses to build cases, pose accusations, or base a right to enforce the curse of sickness and disease, poverty and lack, barrenness, or things like that. Legal things in this context would be anything that will enable the adversary to legally resist, delay, hinder, deny, or even destroy your ability or right to walk in your God-designed, God-created, destiny.

The adversary will use your own unconfessed sin and transgression as a legal case to use against you. He will search your bloodline for unrepented iniquities. He will use your own words, which are legal testimony, against you. He will use the words of people in authority over you directly or the words of people in positions of authority, who sit in spiritual seats and carry authority in the spirit realm because of their office.

He will use anything that carries a voice in the spirit realm that is speaking against you in some way or dimension: your vows, offerings, agreements, contracts, or broken agreements, vows, and covenants. Altars are a major area that can give the adversary legal rights to present a case against you. Altars are places where things are traded or any form of worship takes place.

Our own cleansing, purging, and purifying has as much to do with removing those legal things as it does by just avoiding or stopping some kind of sin or transgression and thinking you're good to go. If the adversary can use it legally, don't think for a moment that he will not try, if it affords him an advantage over you. Second Corinthians 2:10-11 speaks to this.

> *If you freely forgive anyone for anything, then I also forgive him. And if I have forgiven anything, I did so for you before the face of Christ, so that we would not be exploited by the adversary, Satan, for we know his clever schemes* (TPT).

Unforgiveness is one of the favorite things that the adversary uses, that is legal in nature, against us. Unforgiveness is so dangerous that I cannot emphasize the importance of being quick to forgive, no matter what!

In the day of an emphasis on God's grace we need to understand what grace is and what it has provided in the light of the Courts of Heaven. There is an extreme teaching on grace that is leaving people with the idea that because of what God has done where sin is concerned that we can just do whatever we want because God's grace has made us free and all of our sin is forgiven "past, present, and future."

It is true that Jesus dealt with sin, once and for all, and His sacrifice accomplished a Finished Work that does not have to be repeated for any reason for eternity. God has dealt with the sin of Adam and counts the sacrifice of Jesus Christ and the blood He shed as what fulfilled the demands of the Law of Moses. It ended any need for anymore sacrifices; and it did what was necessary for God to be reconciled back to mankind. That is an eternal work that will never, and can never, be repeated.

But the new covenant, instituted by Jesus as High Priest after the order of Melchizedek and ratified by His own blood, has documents that lay out the terms for mankind to enter into that covenant and what kind of life is required to enjoy the full benefits of that covenant. It is not a lawless covenant.

The big difference between the old covenant which had the Law of Moses added to it and the new covenant of God's unconditional love and grace, is that the new covenant provides what the old covenant could never accomplish: the ability of men to be brought into a living union with God through the new birth. This changed everything as far as God was concerned and how He would deal with the born-again new creation believer. It also changed the responsibility of born-again believers and how they are to live their lives and handle sin, transgression, and iniquity; which, by the way, still exist where life in this earth is concerned.

We need to see where the issue of iniquity is still functioning and come to place of recognizing how to stop its influence in our lives. While it is true that God has done everything necessary for us to live free and in victory, the simple truth is that we must take advantage of the finished work of redemption to experience its benefits in a real and tangible way.

Chapter 7

THE MYSTERY OF INIQUITY

The "mystery of iniquity" is something that has been just that, a mystery. This phrase comes from Second Thessalonians 2:7: *"For the mystery of lawlessness is already at work; only He who now restrains will do so until He is taken out of the way."* The word *lawlessness* found here in the New King James Version is translated *iniquity* in the King James Version; it is referring to the underlying principle that is the basis of the spirit of the antichrist.

The Greek word translated as *iniquity* in this verse is *anomia*. Other translations of this word reflect its meaning as described in Strong's Concordance: "illegality, i.e. violation of law or...wickedness:—iniquity, transgress, transgression of the law, unrighteousness."[14] In the New Testament, this word is translated as "iniquity" thirteen times in the King James

Version. Notice that this indicates that iniquity is that which is illegal.

This principle of iniquity is already working and has been working in mankind since the fall of Adam. The reason the word *mystery* is used in relation to it is because satan tries to keep the principle and source of iniquity hidden. And from his perspective, for good reason.

Iniquity is what gives satan the legal right to bring the pressure of temptation in a certain area into a person's life. Because iniquity is illegal activity, it allows the accuser and the adversary to move in a legal way because of illegal activity. Therefore, the temptation to sin, the pressure to commit sin, can come as a result of the legal right granted to the devil by previous generations' illegal spiritual activity.

This is an area that without revelation of the Word and help from the Holy Spirit, you will struggle to maintain a position of victory due to this dimension being hidden. Whatever is hidden, or kept in the dark, cannot be dealt with properly. Sadly, this has been the case with many of the besetting sins and transgressions that are holding Christians in bondage, and the religious treatment of these repetitive behaviors has produced nothing but guilt and condemnation and shame.

It is also reality that the enemy will do all he can to keep hidden the iniquities that give him the legal right to enforce some dimension of the curse in place in our lives and families. This is a real problem when dealing with sickness and disease or other challenging behavioral patterns that can be so frustrating and besetting. Everything from the inability to maintain proper relationships in marriage, which leads to repetitive divorce, to the inability to overcome controlling emotions such as anger, lust, or depression, to dealing with addictions to alcohol, prescription drugs, and pornography are all things that can have some kind of legal issue that makes normal resistance almost futile in securing complete and total victory.

To understand the nature of what we are dealing with, in this chapter I will break down the New Testament revelation that the apostle Paul gives us so that we can gain understanding, and so the light of the Holy Spirit can shine on keys to victory and freedom.

The apostle Paul began to build the foundation of understanding the "mystery of iniquity" in Romans 5 and continues his Holy-Spirit inspired explanation through Romans 8. I will highlight only certain sections of these four chapters to help you to see the nature of the way that the mystery of iniquity works.

I will not repeat what I have already shared about the revelation given us in Romans 5:12-14, except to say that the infection of iniquity entered the entire human race through the fall of Adam. Not one human being born in this planet is immune from this infection, and according to Romans 8:23, that infection was not removed from our physical bodies as a result of the finished work of redemption. Only the hope of redemption of our bodies is granted through the new creation. Hope is futuristic in its orientation; it is not a reality yet.

Therefore, the apostle Paul explains the nature of the problem that this infection poses to the born-again believer. In Romans 5:15-21, he shows how what God was able to accomplish through Jesus, and what He did in the finished work of redemption is far greater in bringing grace, righteousness, and life into our lives than what satan was able to accomplish in bringing sin, condemnation, and death into the human race through Adam's fall.

In Romans 6 we find that once we are born again and receive that abundant grace, we are now in a position that has separated us spiritually from sin, and we need to identify with who we are in Christ where that is concerned and live as those who are dead to sin, but alive unto God.

Substitution and identification are foundational principles that are only introduced through the apostle Paul's writings. Jesus was our substitute, taking our place upon the cross. However, it is how Jesus became our substitute that is so important for us to understand.

He totally identified with us on the cross to the point that He literally became us; He took us into Himself and absorbed our fallen being into His being and became one with us. John 12:32 reveals something that sheds light on this truth. *"And I, if I am lifted up from the earth, will draw all peoples to Myself."*

The phrase *"lifted up"* is always used by Jesus to refer to His crucifixion, being lifted up on the cross. "Lifted up" is translated from the Greek word *helkó*, and in its use in John 12:32 means "to draw by inward power."[15] The best way to illustrate this is what you can observe by placing a completely dry sponge, with absolutely no moisture content, In a dish or bowl of water. The sponge will absorb all the water, up to its maximum capacity to do so. Jesus absorbed all of mankind into Himself on the cross and had the capacity to do so because He was the second person of the Godhead.

It was at that moment that we were made one with Christ legally. The legal side of redemption was initiated in the Garden of Gethsemane and was not fully completed until Jesus sat down at the right hand of majesty on high and took His place as the mediator between God and man. Once His blood was applied to the mercy seat in the heavenly holy of holies, and as high priest after the order of Melchizedek, He sat down to administrate the legal dimension of the new covenant, there was nothing left undone legally with respect to restoring God's side of the relationship with man. The only thing left undone was what man would have to do to vitally experience the full benefits of all that God, through Christ, had accomplished.

We were in Christ on that cross, and in Him and through Him we were made alive to God and died to spiritual death and the power of sin, legally. However, this is not experienced in its fullness automatically in our everyday life experience in this earth, even after we receive Jesus as Lord. The new birth puts us into position spiritually to legally enforce and execute into place all that the verdict of the finished work of redemption secured for us. Without being born again, we do not have that legal right.

Our identification with Christ and using all that He made available for us from a legal position is an absolute vital place from which we must function to experience the full benefits for which He suffered, died, was resurrected, and ascended to provide. It is interesting that in studying the meaning of the Greek word *helkó*, I discovered that it is akin to the Greek word *haireó*, which means "to choose."[16]

Jesus *chose* to accomplish the will of the Father by going to the cross. He chose to absorb us into Himself; it was not something He was forced to do. This is why we must make the choice to become one with Him. We must receive Him and what He accomplished for us; it is not automatically imposed on us, even though it is God's will and great desire for us. Love always leaves us a choice.

Romans 6:19 is an important verse for us to grasp at this point in our understanding. *"I speak in human terms because of the weakness of your flesh. For just as you presented your members as slaves of uncleanness, and of lawlessness leading to more lawlessness, so now present your members as slaves of righteousness for holiness."* Again the King James version uses the word *iniquity* for *lawlessness*. Thus, "iniquity leading to more iniquity" gives us some insight.

Iniquity is generational in its effects. It can be passed down from one generation to the next. It opens the door for certain sins to be repeated over and over within family lines to such a point that the iniquity shapes the family identity over time. At that point it is both a mind-set and a genetic predisposition. No one has to teach iniquity; it is unlearned behavior that the predisposition has already been genetically programmed as a result of the generation dimension of sin started by Adam.

An example of this from the Old Testament will reveal the generational aspect of iniquity. This can be found in three generations beginning with Abraham. Two times prior to Isaac's birth, Abraham lied about Sarah being his sister, rather than telling truth that she was his wife. The first time was when he and Sarah went down to Egypt when a famine hit the land of Canaan. This is recorded in Genesis 12:10-20.

Now there was a famine in the land, and Abram went down to Egypt to dwell there, for the famine was severe in the land. And it came to pass, when he was close to entering Egypt, that he said to Sarai his wife, "Indeed I know that you are a woman of beautiful countenance. Therefore it will happen, when the Egyptians see you, that they will say, 'This is his wife'; and they will kill me, but they will let you live. Please say you are my sister, that it may be well with me for your sake, and that I may live because of you."

So it was, when Abram came into Egypt, that the Egyptians saw the woman, that she was very beautiful. The princes of Pharaoh also saw her and commended her to Pharaoh. And the woman was taken to Pharaoh's house. He treated Abram well for her sake. He had sheep, oxen, male donkeys, male and female servants, female donkeys, and camels.

But the Lord plagued Pharaoh and his house with great plagues because of Sarai, Abram's wife. And

Pharaoh called Abram and said, "What is this you have done to me? Why did you not tell me that she was your wife? Why did you say, 'She is my sister'? I might have taken her as my wife. Now therefore, here is your wife; take her and go your way." So Pharaoh commanded his men concerning him; and they sent him away, with his wife and all that he had.

The second time Abraham did this is recorded in Genesis 20:1-14.

And Abraham journeyed from there to the South, and dwelt between Kadesh and Shur, and stayed in Gerar. Now Abraham said of Sarah his wife, "She is my sister." And Abimelech king of Gerar sent and took Sarah.

But God came to Abimelech in a dream by night, and said to him, "Indeed you are a dead man because of the woman whom you have taken, for she is a man's wife."

But Abimelech had not come near her; and he said, "Lord, will You slay a righteous nation also? Did he not say to me, 'She is my sister'? And she, even she herself said, 'He is my brother.' In the integrity of my heart and innocence of my hands I have done this."

And God said to him in a dream, "Yes, I know that you did this in the integrity of your heart. For I also withheld you from sinning against Me; therefore I did not let you touch her. Now therefore, restore the man's wife; for he is a prophet, and he will pray for you and you shall live. But if you do not restore her, know that you shall surely die, you and all who are yours."

So Abimelech rose early in the morning, called all his servants, and told all these things in their hearing; and the men were very much afraid. And Abimelech called Abraham and said to him, "What have you done to us? How have I offended you, that you have brought on me and on my kingdom a great sin? You have done deeds to me that ought not to be done." Then Abimelech said to Abraham, "What did you have in view, that you have done this thing?"

And Abraham said, "Because I thought, surely the fear of God is not in this place; and they will kill me on account of my wife. But indeed she is truly my sister. She is the daughter of my father, but not the daughter of my mother; and she became my wife. And it came to pass, when God caused me to wander from my father's house, that I said to her, 'This is your kindness that you should do for me: in every place, wherever we go, say of me, "He is my brother."'"

Then Abimelech took sheep, oxen, and male and female servants, and gave them to Abraham; and he restored Sarah his wife to him.

Now, after having read these two accounts of a pattern of lying about the relationship with Sarah, take notice that all of this happened prior to the birth of Isaac. So, there is no way that Isaac could have learned to lie in this manner by observation, nor would it be likely that Abraham would have taught Isaac to do this kind of thing.

Lying was a sin in that day just as it is now. The only difference is that God was not imputing sin to Abraham's account (as revealed in Romans 5:12-14). Abraham was actually having his faith accounted to him for righteousness (as shown in Genesis 15:6; Romans 4:3; Galatians 3:6; James 2:23). So, God was not holding the sin of lying against Abraham, but it did start a generational pattern that showed up in next in Isaac.

Pay close attention to this passage from Genesis 26:1-14 and see if you catch the iniquity of Abraham showing up in Isaac's behavior.

> *There was a famine in the land, besides the first famine that was in the days of Abraham. And Isaac went to Abimelech king of the Philistines, in Gerar. Then the Lord appeared to him and said: "Do not go down to Egypt; live in the land of which I shall tell you. Dwell in this land, and I will be with you and bless you; for to you and your descendants I give all these lands, and I will perform the oath which I swore to Abraham your father. And I will make your descendants multiply as the stars of heaven; I will give to your descendants all these lands; and in your seed all the nations of the earth shall be blessed; because Abraham obeyed My voice and kept My charge, My commandments, My statutes, and My laws."*
>
> *So Isaac dwelt in Gerar. And the men of the place asked about his wife. And he said, "She is my sister";*

for he was afraid to say, "She is my wife," because he thought, "lest the men of the place kill me for Rebekah, because she is beautiful to behold." Now it came to pass, when he had been there a long time, that Abimelech king of the Philistines looked through a window, and saw, and there was Isaac, showing endearment to Rebekah his wife. Then Abimelech called Isaac and said, "Quite obviously she is your wife; so how could you say, 'She is my sister'?" Isaac said to him, "Because I said, 'Lest I die on account of her.'"

And Abimelech said, "What is this you have done to us? One of the people might soon have lain with your wife, and you would have brought guilt on us." So Abimelech charged all his people, saying, "He who touches this man, or his wife shall surely be put to death."

Then Isaac sowed in that land, and reaped in the same year a hundredfold; and the Lord blessed him. The man began to prosper, and continued prospering until he became very prosperous; for he had possessions of flocks and possessions of herds and a great number of servants. So the Philistines envied him.

You can see that Isaac repeated the same behavior that his father, Abraham, demonstrated in exactly the same situation. This was not coincidence; it is bloodline iniquity at work. God didn't tell Abraham to lie, nor did He instruct Isaac to lie. God is not the father of lying! Jesus revealed lying originated from satan (see John 8:44).

This iniquity made the relationship with kings somewhat more difficult than it should have been. And in the case of Abimelech, it almost got him into serious trouble with God.

It is also important to note that even after lying to Abimelech, Isaac experienced the blessing of the Lord on his crops during a famine to the degree that he received a hundredfold in the same year in which he sowed, which was a year of famine.

One last observation to make before we go the next example of this sin going into the next generation. Notice what the Lord said to Isaac about his father, Abraham, in verses 4 and 5.

> *And I will make your descendants multiply as the stars of heaven; I will give to your descendants all these lands; and in your seed all the nations of the earth shall be blessed; because Abraham obeyed My voice and kept My charge, My commandments, My statutes, and My laws.*

This is very interesting in that we know that Abraham lied twice, but God said that he had been obedient to God's voice, and had kept God's charge, commandments, statues, and laws. Understand that this was said at least four hundred years before the Law of Moses was given on Mount Sinai. Sin cannot be imputed by God when there is no law to reveal sin.

Abraham, the father of faith, was far from a perfect human being. He believed and obeyed God, and that was what allowed God to treat him as if sin had never existed. However, the sins and iniquity that were passed on from one generation to the next would one day need to be dealt with, for the wages of sin is death.

We have seen the sin of Abraham and the sin of Isaac. Did it continue to the next generation? We see something interesting in Isaac's sons where this is concerned. When Rebekah was pregnant with twins, she inquired of the Lord concerning them because they seemed to be fighting within the womb. We find the Lord's response in Genesis 25:23.

> *And the Lord said to her: "Two nations are in your womb, two peoples shall be separated from your body; one people shall be stronger than the other, and the older shall serve the younger."*

We know that the two sons were Jacob and Esau. The name Jacob means supplanter, layer of snares. Jacob took advantage of Esau's hunger and traded a bowl of food for the birthright of the firstborn (see Gen. 25:27-34). Later, with Rebekah's help, Jacob deceived his father, even lying about his identity, convincing Isaac that he was Esau. Jacob received the blessing of the firstborn (Gen. 27:1-40). True to his name, and in the full influence of the bloodline iniquity that began with his grandfather Abraham, Jacob supplanted the firstborn birthright and blessing from Esau.

In Romans 7 the apostle Paul explains the nature of sin in the flesh and how this infection that began in Adam wars against the mind and the spirit. He is writing this not explaining how sin works in the sinner who is not born again, but as the man who was miraculously changed on the road to

Damascus, as a new creation believer, as an apostle of God. So read this section beginning in verse 15 through verse 25 with that in mind.

> *For what I am doing, I do not understand. For what I will to do, that I do not practice; but what I hate, that I do. If, then, I do what I will not to do, I agree with the law that it is good. But now, it is no longer I who do it, but sin that dwells in me. For I know that in me (that is, in my flesh) nothing good dwells; for to will is present with me, but how to perform what is good I do not find. For the good that I will to do, I do not do; but the evil I will not to do, that I practice. Now if I do what I will not to do, it is no longer I who do it, but sin that dwells in me. I find then a law, that evil is present with me, the one who wills to do good. For I delight in the law of God according to the inward man. But I see another law in my members, warring against the law of my mind, and bringing me into captivity to the law of sin which is in my members. O wretched man that I am! Who will deliver me from this body of death? I thank God—through Jesus Christ our Lord! So then, with the mind I myself serve the law of God, but with the flesh the law of sin.*

Paul is explaining the nature of this infection that is in all our physical bodies, this infection of sin that came from Adam. Verse 17 is a key verse for us to understand: *"But now, it is no longer I who do it, but sin that dwells in me."*

108

In order to sin, the born again believer must yield to the pressure of the flesh that comes from the infection of sin in the flesh. After you are born again, your spirit is a new creation and is indwelt with the Holy Spirit. There are some other New Testament verses to plug into our understanding here. First let's look at Galatians 5:16-18.

> *I say then: Walk in the Spirit, and you shall not fulfill the lust of the flesh. For the flesh lusts against the Spirit, and the Spirit against the flesh; and these are contrary to one another, so that you do not do the things that you wish. But if you are led by the Spirit, you are not under the law.*

The flesh puts pressure on your born-again spirit, and your born-again spirit pushes back against the pressure of the fleshly passions. This dynamic is what must be controlled, and the key to winning that battle is twofold.

The first step that must become a discipline in the life of anyone who is a born-again believer is to renew the mind to your new identity in Christ. The revelation of who you are in Christ and who Christ is in you, and all that living union affords you in rights, ability, authority, and power, is an absolute must for winning the battle over the pressure of the flesh.

What we did not know until the revelation of the Courts of Heaven began to be unveiled to the Body of Christ is how to deal with the unbearable pressure of iniquity in the bloodline that gives a legal right to the adversary to keep the pressure on until the flesh wins out over the resistance of the spirit. This ability to use time as a weapon and keep unrelenting pressure on the mind and will until a person caves is another dimension of the mystery of iniquity that can now be successfully dealt with so that victory can be obtained.

Let's add another section of New Testament truth to our understanding. Look at James 1:12-15.

> *Blessed is the man who endures temptation; for when he has been approved, he will receive the crown of life which the Lord has promised to those who love Him. Let no one say when he is tempted, "I am tempted by God"; for God cannot be tempted by evil, nor does He Himself tempt anyone. But each one is tempted when he is drawn away by his own desires and enticed. Then, when desire has conceived, it gives birth to sin; and sin, when it is full-grown, brings forth death.*

The first thing to notice here is that temptation can have an element of time connected to it. The word *endures* is indicative of having to stand against something for a span of time.

Another important point to take note of is that temptation is not coming from God. God may *test* us. But He will never *tempt* us. God will never use anything evil or anything from the curse to tempt us. James goes on to identify where the temptation is coming from and it agrees with what the apostle Paul spoke of in Romans 7.

> *When you are tempted don't ever say, "God is tempting me," for God is incapable of being tempted by evil and he is never the source of temptation. Instead it is*

*each person's own desires and thoughts that drag them
into evil and lure them away into darkness* (James
1:13-14 TPT).

Your own lusts, desires, and passions of the flesh are the
source of temptation. It is that infection of sin, the inheritance
from Adam, that rises up to gain influence over your mind and
will. And as James goes on to describe, yielding to the pressure
and obeying the flesh will lead to things that are manifestations of the law of sin and death spoken of in Romans 8.

The apostle John identifies the three main avenues of
temptation that we must be aware of on a constant basis. We
find this in First John 2:16: *"For all that is in the world—the
lust of the flesh, the lust of the eyes, and the pride of life—is not of
the Father but is of the world."*

Pressure produced from the desires, appetites, and passions of the flesh; the desires, appetites, and passions that are
inflamed by the sight of our eyes; and the pride of life, which
is self-will (or may we identify it this way: iniquity), are not
from the Father. They come from the world and its culture of
sin and death as well as from the bloodline iniquities that give
the adversary a legal right to tempt us to sin.

We can now go back to Romans 7 and have some better
understanding of what the apostle Paul is explaining for us.

> *But I see another law in my members, warring against
> the law of my mind, and bringing me into captivity
> to the law of sin which is in my members. O wretched
> man that I am! Who will deliver me from this body of*

111

death? I thank God—through Jesus Christ our Lord!
So then, with the mind I myself serve the law of God,
but with the flesh the law of sin (vv. 23-25).

Notice that he says this law of sin is warring against the law of the mind. And Paul declares that Jesus Christ is the one who will deliver us from this body of death. But we need to understand how to take advantage of what Jesus has provided and then properly execute the legal right of deliverance into place in our lives so that we experience the freedom He has purchased for us.

We find a legal decree, based upon the verdict of the cross stated as clearly as possible in Romans 8:2: *"For the law of the Spirit of life in Christ Jesus has made me free from the law of sin and death."*

We must learn how to actually execute that verdict into place in our lives so that freedom can become our reality. I want to explain what this means so that it makes sense to you.

When a court tries a case, the jury (if it is a trial by jury) or the judge will determine the verdict. Once the verdict has been rendered, the next step is a judgment (decision) is made, and at that point the officers of the court will see to it that the verdict is executed into place by enforcing the judgment. The judge will not do that job; it is up to those with the authority to execute the verdict and carry out the judgment to see that justice is served.

Verdicts can be challenged and judgments can be overturned, if someone determines that there is enough evidence to support the legal right to fight the outcome of the court.

Where we see this playing out almost every day in many nations around the world is in matters of inheritance law. Probate court is probably the closest example to what we have to deal with in spiritual conflicts that are legal in nature.

As I have already touched on earlier, the legal things that the adversary uses to keep us from walking in the manifestation of what we already have been provided in Christ have to do with things that we have a responsibility and authority to deal with through our union with Christ. God is not our problem; He is on our side!

The adversary cannot "take" our inheritance away from us spiritually; his attempts to thwart our inheritance has to do with us walking in the physical manifestation of it in this earth where it demonstrates Jesus's lordship over the kingdom of darkness. It does not matter, in any way, if he stops this in the courtroom or on the battlefield; he just wants it stopped!

I want to reinforce the importance of keeping your own personal sins and transgressions from lingering in a realm where the adversary can use them as legal issues against you. First John 1:9 is the way you avoid that kind of a legal situation. And here is why this is important in the light of what we are discussing in this book.

In your spirit as a new creation, you are holy and righteous. God is not sin-conscious where you are concerned. However, as we have seen from Romans 8:23, your physical body is not redeemed; it is corrupt, weak, and carries the infection of iniquity that has been passed down generationally from Adam. These are the things that can be a legal accusation and case that the adversary uses to legally hinder, delay, or deny your enjoying your inheritance in the earth.

Bloodline iniquity does not hinder your fellowship with God. Personal sin and transgression will. You cannot walk in darkness and have fellowship with the light. First John 1:5-6 is clear.

> *This is the message which we have heard from Him and declare to you, that God is light and in Him is no darkness at all. If we say that we have fellowship with Him, and walk in darkness, we lie and do not practice the truth.*

Add to this what we read in Second Corinthians 6, the last part of verse 14: *"And what communion has light with darkness?"* It is readily understood that light and darkness cannot commune (fellowship) with each other. For the believer to think that he can live in sin without it hindering his fellowship with God is to be deceived. Sin doesn't affect your relationship with God, but it will definitely affect your intimacy with God. First John 1:9 has absolutely nothing to do with restoring relationship with God; it has everything to do with restoring fellowship and intimacy with God.

It also is how you "fix your case" with Jesus so that the adversary cannot use your own sin and transgression against you. One further point that needs to be understood in this regard. Look at First John 1:8: *"If we say that we have no sin, we deceive ourselves, and the truth is not in us."* And take a look at verse 10: *"If we say that we have not sinned, we make Him a liar, and His word is not in us."*

A careful breakdown of verse 8 will show that the apostle John is addressing the sin nature in this verse. If you say that you have no sin nature, you are deceived! You also are essentially accusing God of lying. The sin nature is in your flesh, and it is why your flesh is corrupt and weak. Its passions war against the desires of your spirit. That war takes place in your mind.

The "battlefield" with which we conduct the majority of our warfare is spiritual only to the extent that our fleshly passions are being energized by the influence of demonic entities that put thoughts and images in our minds. These satanically aligned spiritual entities are very subtle in the way they operate, and they can be very persistent.

It is the sin nature already resident in our body that makes fear such a powerful weapon in the hands of our enemy. Because these spirits are unseen and know how to operate with skill and cunning craftiness against the human race, they are extremely effective in soliciting responses of either behavior or words, or even both; revealing to them that their strategies are working.

It is this sin nature, sown with generational iniquities, that the enemy will use against us as we become greater governmental threats to his affairs. This is especially true when he is looking for a way to take out a spiritually mature believer who is learning how to walk in love and use faith and authority in Christ to greater effectiveness against him. In the beginning this level of strategy is not so much a battlefield in the mind as it is a legal maneuver designed to use time as a weapon against a strong believer who is walking in a greater level of faith. This is also where the "spiritual warfare" mind-set has blinded people of even great faith, and experience and success has been more difficult to secure.

After many weeks, months, and then years go by battling symptoms, circumstances, and repetitive behaviors, none of which are indicating any weakening, and can even be getting worse, even strong believers begin to deal with the mental battles as the demonic spirits assigned to their case ramp up the pressure. Fear becomes a very real mental and emotional pressure that has to be dealt with on an ever-increasing basis.

With time passing, the physical struggles (especially in the case of a debilitating disease), the mental and emotional struggles (as can be so real in financial and relationship circumstances), and the overall weariness of the entire situation begins to tear away at the will, to weaken it, and bring a person to a point of giving up. Add to this the frustration of not getting prayers answered and wondering where or when God will move and why He has not already moved to bring deliverance and you can see the problem.

This is why what I described in the introduction of this book is playing out in so many situations. Something legal has been used by the adversary to introduce delay, and the result of this delay is deferred hope. Proverbs 13:12 reveals this clearly. *"Hope deferred makes the heart sick, but when the desire comes, it is a tree of life."*

This is what the enemy is after. And he is a master at extending the battle. His motive is to wear believers out and put pressure on them and keep it on until they give up and quit, or the disease finally destroys their body's ability to sustain life. Daniel 7:25 shows that this is one of the enemy's strategies.

> *He will speak out against the Most High and wear down the saints of the Highest One, and he will intend to make alterations in times and in law; and they will be given into his hand for a time, times, and half a time* (NASB).

Spiritual warfare alone cannot and will not turn this around; the casualty rate in the Body of Christ is proving this to be the case. I want to emphasize that it is happening not because we have been taught wrong; it is because we haven't known all there is to know about how our enemy is able to work against us. Hosea 4:6 applies in this case.

> *My people are destroyed for lack of knowledge. Because you have rejected knowledge, I also will reject you from being priest for Me; because you have forgotten the law of your God, I also will forget your children.*

Notice it is not just a lack of knowledge that creates a problem. Rejecting knowledge has consequences that have to do with functioning as a priest, which is particularly important to the ability of believers being able to function in the Courts of Heaven. We function in the courts as priests, dealing with the legal issues that have to be handled to bring results in so many of the situations we can find ourselves in on a day-to-day basis.

Forgetting knowledge of God's Word also creates problems that can show up in the enemy being able to take advantage of our children. We have to understand that we are not just living our lives for ourselves; we are responsible to secure a better life spiritually for our children as well. It is not going to happen automatically.

This brings me back to First John and what verse 10 is addressing. *"If we say that we have not sinned, we make Him a liar, and His word is not in us."*

In this verse, the apostle John is dealing with the idea that our present sins and transgressions are not an issue of concern. If you say that you have not sinned, when you have and haven't dealt with them according to First John 1:9, you are setting yourself up for problems that you cannot even imagine.

There is no such thing as living in sinless perfection in this life. No one can. I don't care how mature and well developed in the faith you become, no one can say they have not sinned. This level of deception is dangerous. While there may be a few believers that think this way, the extreme grace teaching of modern times has produced another attitude that is just as dangerous and can be deadly.

That attitude is expressed this way: *Well, since God has already forgiven me of my sins, past, present, and future, I don't have to confess my sins. I am already forgiven. I can do whatever I want, and God has already forgiven me.*

This thinking flies in the face of so many strong instructions in the New Testament letters that I don't have the time nor space to deal with in this book. I will just say this again.

God has dealt with the entire world's sin problem through the sacrifice of Jesus on the cross. That satisfied the Law of Moses where sacrifice is concerned and enabled God to be reconciled to the world, once and for all.

He is not *imputing* sins now (see 2 Cor. 5:19). He is not reckoning, or marking to anyone's account, all the individual sins on a one-by-one basis for the entire world. There is actually only one sin that the Holy Spirit is convicting the world of at this moment: the sin of unbelief (see John 16:8-9).

For believers, the realization of our inability to completely live free from sin in this life is fully covered in the first two chapters of First John. The breakdown is described in a brief summary for this book, as I understand it.

First John 1:7 reveals that if we walk in the light (the revelation of the truth that we have), there is ongoing fellowship between God and us, as well as, between believers who are walking in the same light. When this is the case, the blood of Jesus is cleansing us of sin we may be unknowingly committing.

> *But if we walk in the light as He is in the light, we have fellowship with one another, and the blood of Jesus Christ His Son cleanses us from all sin.*

The dynamic of what is unknown sin is one that cannot be even judged properly or justly on the human level because we are all at different levels of understanding and maturity. As you grow in Christ, the measure of what is sin where you are concerned will change because greater knowledge and light demands a different standard. God, in any case, is not going to hold you responsible for attitudes and behaviors that He counts as sin but that you are not aware are an issue. Only when He deals with you on a certain point do you then become responsible.

When you sin and know it, First John 1:9 is the way you handle it. In your function as a priest before God, it is your responsibility (as we have already shown from First John 3:3; Second Corinthians 7:1; and Second Timothy 2:19-21) to cleanse yourself from defilement that can disrupt your fellowship with the Father as well as introduce a legal issue that the adversary and accuser can exploit against you.

> *If we confess our sins, He is faithful and just to forgive us our sins and to cleanse us from all unrighteousness* (1 John 1:9).

In First John 2:1-6 we read some very important words.

> *My little children, these things I write to you, so that you may not sin. And if anyone sins, we have an Advocate with the Father, Jesus Christ the righteous. And He Himself is the propitiation for our sins, and not for ours only but also for the whole world. Now by this we know that we know Him, if we keep His commandments. He who says, "I know Him," and does not keep His commandments, is a liar, and the truth is not in him. But whoever keeps His word, truly the love of God is perfected in him. By this we know that we are in Him. He who says he abides in Him ought himself also to walk just as He walked.*

We can see that the apostle John is concerned that any attitude of treating sin lightly would be discouraged. This alone should give pause to any idea that we can live a life of sin after we are born again with no thought as to the consequences. We have to remember that the apostle Paul was the one who revealed by the Holy Spirit's inspiration that sin leads to death. Romans 6:20-23 is as clear on this as you can get.

> *For when you were slaves of sin, you were free in regard to righteousness. What fruit did you have then in the things of which you are now ashamed? For the end of those things is death. But now having been set free from sin, and having become slaves of God, you have your fruit to holiness, and the end, everlasting life. For the wages of sin is death, but the gift of God is eternal life in Christ Jesus our Lord.*

Born again or not, sin will bring death into play in your life. Sickness, disease, financial trouble, stress and anxiety, and many other dimensions of incipient death all are either directly, or indirectly, connected to unrepented sin. There is no such thing as sinning without consequences. At the very least, sin will complicate your life in ways that create a lot of needless pain. (We have already mentioned James 1:15, which shows again that the end result of sin is death.) The only way to limit the effects of sin is to handle it properly, which is what John is addressing.

First John 2:1-2 communicates the apostle John's purpose for writing—that we would not sin. Knowing that we all can and do sin, he reveals the important truth that Jesus Christ is our advocate with the Father. Jesus, who is the Righteous Judge, is also our legal assistant to get things taken care of with the Father when we break fellowship as a result of sin.

> *My little children, these things I write to you, so that you may not sin. And if anyone sins, we have an Advocate with the Father, Jesus Christ the righteous. And He Himself is the propitiation for our sins, and not for ours only but also for the whole world.*

It is important to note that the sacrifice that Jesus made to propitiate for our sins was not for just the born-again believer, but also for the entire world. The unbeliever enters into relationship with the Father through Jesus Christ; the believer restores fellowship through the same sacrifice. The finished work of redemption covers it all.

There is one last great passage of Scripture that needs to be shared to bring understanding to our minds and hearts with respect to God's perspective on our sins and iniquities. Let's take a look at the following verses from Hebrews 10:14-22.

> *For by one offering He has perfected forever those who are being sanctified. But the Holy Spirit also witnesses to us; for after He had said before, "This is the covenant that I will make with them after those days, says the Lord: I will put My laws into their hearts, and in their minds, I will write them," then He adds, "Their sins and their lawless deeds I will remember no more." Now where there is remission of these, there is no longer an offering for sin. Therefore, brethren,*

having boldness to enter the Holiest by the blood of Jesus, by a new and living way which He consecrated for us, through the veil, that is, His flesh, and having a High Priest over the house of God, let us draw near with a true heart in full assurance of faith, having our hearts sprinkled from an evil conscience and our bodies washed with pure water.

The Father has never known you and me as sinners. His commitment to what He predestined for us in our individual books of destiny is the way that He sees us. When we get born again through union with Christ, we enter into relationship with God based upon the gift of righteousness that is ours through oneness with Christ. It is a work of grace and is completed in our lives when we believe in Jesus.

Jesus is the high priest, the mediator between God and man, and as the second person of the Godhead, is able to function as our Righteous Judge and deal with our broken fellowship with the Father by doing what He alone can do in the position of high priest and judge. This is why our confession of sin is so important to maintaining fellowship and taking advantage of our union with Jesus as high priest. I want to say this again. Our sin doesn't affect our righteousness; our sin does affect fellowship. We are able to deal with those occasional times we miss it and restore fellowship because we remain in a position of righteousness.

Bloodline iniquity does not affect our righteousness or our fellowship; it only gives the adversary something legal to use against us to hinder our ability to walk in and manifest our inheritance in Christ in this earth, or delay and possibly deny us from walking in greater measures of our book of destiny. The greater threat you become governmentally to the enemy, the more likely he is to search out legal things to try and stop you from fulfilling your purpose and destiny, because if he doesn't do something to deter you, he knows your success will result in hastening his day of reckoning.

The Father is not the one bringing these things up; and Jesus, as our Righteous Judge, will not pervert judgment when the adversary brings a legal accusation or case against us. Since all the bloodline iniquities are things attached to our unredeemed body's ancestral history, we have to answer those matters in the court and get them removed. This is another area where our relationship with Jesus and the Holy Spirit is of such great importance.

I want to bring to your attention this example from Luke 22:31-32 to show you where Peter learned about the strategy of the devil functioning as an adversary and how Jesus was the one who handled his case.

> *And the Lord said, "Simon, Simon! Indeed, Satan has asked for you, that he may sift you as wheat. But I have prayed for you, that your faith should not fail; and when you have returned to Me, strengthen your brethren."*

The word *asked* in the New King James Version is the Greek word *exaitéomai*, which literally means "to demand (for trial)."[17] The phrase "sift you as wheat" comes from the Greek *siniázō* which is defined as "by inward agitation to try one's faith to the verge of overthrow."[18] Putting these two words together, we find that satan has demanded Peter be turned over for a trial in court for the purpose of putting so much pressure on Peter by inward agitation to try to overthrow Peter's faith. The adversary had found something legal by which he intended to overthrow Peter's faith and get him to do the same thing that Judas did. But Jesus prayed for Peter and was able to get a judgment that would not allow the adversary to push Peter to commit suicide. He did deny the Lord three times, but he was eventually restored back to fellowship with Jesus after His resurrection.

Chapter 8

THE NATURE OF BLOODLINE INIQUITY

I want to delve further into the nature of bloodline iniquity so that you can understand how to recognize when it may be functioning in your life or in your family. There are signposts and indicators that are characteristics of iniquity that may be a bloodline issue.

In my experience of doing court cases for myself and for others, I can say with all confidence that what has been commonly called "generational curses" are the symptoms of a greater root, and that would be iniquity.

Proverbs 26:2 is clear that the curse cannot land without a legal right or cause.

Curses will not harm someone who is innocent; they are like sparrows or swallows that fly around and never land (NCV).

You can actually get delivered of a curse personally, and yet without realizing that it may be manifesting due to a legal right in the bloodline, see the same thing show up in other members of the family. We want to remove the legal right for the curse to land from the family so that it cannot touch the family ever again.

I have seen this play out in so many families, and I have seen the frustration and heartache that a curse connected to bloodline iniquity can bring by affecting successive generations, or multiple members of a family, even after one person was delivered by a miracle or by taking a strong stand of personal faith. When you get rid of the legal right for the curse to keep manifesting; which is the bloodline iniquity, the entire family will go free.

I am reminded at this juncture of the declaration that the apostle Paul made to the Philippian jailor as recorded in Acts 16:31: *"Believe on the Lord Jesus Christ, and you will be saved, you and your household."* God does not want to bring salvation to this world one person at a time; He wants to save whole households at a time!

From Adam's fall until the birth of Jesus, God had to protect the integrity of the righteous bloodline from which Mary would come from to keep the adversary from having a legal claim on her bloodline. This was why the prohibitions against entering into covenants with the heathen nations was so important, and it was why idolatry and cultism that came from the influence of the heathen nations around Israel brought such harsh judgment.

As we have shown in an earlier chapter, blood is a powerful spiritual property, both for blessing and for empowering the curse. When you read the early chapters of the Book of Genesis, you have to keep in mind that the promise made to satan vicariously functioning through the serpent in Genesis 3:15 was behind another dimension of the purpose of the Law of Moses; it was to put the boundaries up to protect the righteous bloodline from which the virgin Mary would come. Any legal claim by the adversary on that bloodline, introduced by iniquity, would have disqualified the bloodline.

The biggest qualifier was faith in God, which we learn from the New Testament letters, was what God needed to count the Old Testament believer as righteous. This was the main spiritual quality that kept the righteous bloodline free from legal claims by the adversary.

As I mentioned in the introduction, it has long been understood from the visions of Daniel that there is a Court in Heaven, and that court convenes over matters that pertain to the Kingdom of God. Take another look at this from Daniel 7:9-10.

> *I watched till thrones were put in place, and the Ancient of Days was seated; His garment was white as snow, and the hair of His head was like pure wool. His throne was a fiery flame, its wheels a burning fire; a fiery stream issued and came forth from before*

Him. A thousand thousands ministered to Him; ten
thousand times ten thousand stood before Him. The
court was seated, and the books were opened.

Verses 21 and 22 reveal the nature of the business of the
Court of Heaven as it relates to what Daniel was seeing in
the vision.

I was watching; and the same horn was making war
against the saints, and prevailing against them, until
the Ancient of Days came, and a judgment was made
in favor of the saints of the Most High, and the time
came for the saints to possess the kingdom.

As the vision continues, we see the outcome of the action
of the court, which gives us insight as to the nature of the
legal power of the court and the fact that once the court comes
to a ruling and issues a judgment, governmental authority is
released to God's people and they are able to rule in the earth
in greater measures with little or no resistance.

He shall speak pompous words against the Most High,
shall persecute the saints of the Most High, and shall
intend to change times and law. Then the saints shall
be given into his hand for a time and times and half
a time.

But the court shall be seated, and they shall take away
his dominion, to consume and destroy it forever. Then
the kingdom and dominion, and the greatness of the
kingdoms under the whole heaven, shall be given to
the people, the saints of the Most High. His kingdom

is an everlasting kingdom, and all dominions shall serve and obey Him (vv. 25-27).

However you interpret these passages in the light of your understanding of the end times does not change the reality revealed in these verses. The Court of Heaven exists to secure God's prophetic intentions and assist His people to accomplish their part in the earth, based upon what has been written in the legal books of Heaven.

I might add here that the ultimate purpose of the Courts of Heaven is to remove the legal claims that the devil has on cities, states, regions, and nations as the Body of Christ steps into its priestly position at the right hand of the Father and functions with the Righteous Judge, Jesus Christ, to take possession of its inheritance purchased through the finished work of redemption.

Every one of the legal claims that the devil uses to keep that from happening are matters relating to what was legally handed over to him by Adam when Adam sinned (Luke 4:5-6). Those legal claims cannot be dealt with through battlefield tactics. They have to be secured first by the Body of Christ doing the work in the Court of Heaven and then with the authority invested in them by the head of the Church, executing the verdicts and carrying out the judgments of the court in the earth. This pattern is reflected in how Jesus is described in Revelation 19:11: *"Now I saw heaven opened, and behold, a white horse. And He who sat on him was called Faithful and True, and in righteousness He judges and makes war."*

From His place of righteousness, that place of being in perfect oneness with the Father, Jesus judges (carries out judicial activity from the Court of Heaven) and makes war (executes the verdicts and judgments secured in the court into place), carrying out those legal matters to full completion in the earth.

The earthly contingent of His Body, born-again believers, are the ones working with Jesus in the courtroom as priests and then function as kings in the earth to enforce the rulings of the court. The actions of the Court of Heaven are to precede the activity in the earth that would effectively carry out the judgments of the court and execute verdicts into place.

Many times manifestations of the curse do not respond to attempts to exercise authority by believers because the necessary work to remove the legal issues that cause the curse to function has not been done. Our authority is delegated and does not work at our initiative, any more than Jesus's authority as Son of Man while in the earth functioned at His initiative. Nothing, and I mean *nothing*, initiates in the Kingdom of God at man's initiative when it comes to releasing authority. This is because man is not the source of the authority, God is.

Ambassadors, in and of themselves, carry no authority. The authority of ambassadors function only when they have been given the words to speak and the actions to take that originated with the head of the government that they represent. Any words and actions of ambassadors that originate from them alone, or at their own initiative, carry absolutely no legal authority. The governments they represent are under no obligation to back self-willed words and actions of ambassadors.

Jesus indicated this same level of delegated authority is how things work under His headship over the Body of Christ. Look at what He said in John 15:4-5.

> *Abide in Me, and I in you.* ***As the branch cannot bear fruit of itself, unless it abides in the vine,*** *neither can you, unless you abide in Me. I am the vine, you are the branches. He who abides in Me, and I in him, bears much fruit;* ***for without Me you can do nothing.***

To abide means "to live in organic oneness with." This entails a constant state of fellowship where we as members of Jesus's Body are only acting and speaking at the impulses that originate from the head. Any self-willed actions or words on our part do not obligate the head in any form or fashion. Even Jesus did not act or speak in a way that was self-willed. The reason is because self-will is iniquity.

I gave you the following verses of Scripture earlier in this book, but I need to repeat them here for emphasis of this major point concerning self-will being iniquity, which is a major legal issue that the adversary will seize upon to his advantage.

> *So Jesus said, "I speak to you timeless truth. The Son is not able to do anything from himself or through my own initiative. I only do the works that I see the Father doing, for the Son does the same works as his Father"* (John 5:19 TPT).
>
> *I can do nothing on My own initiative. As I hear, I judge; and My judgment is just, because I do not*

seek My own will, but the will of Him who sent Me (John 5:30 NASB).

For I have come down from Heaven, not to do what I want, but to do the will of him who sent me (John 6:38 PNT).

My teaching does not belong to me, but comes from Him who sent me (John 7:16 WNT).

"I have many things to speak and to judge concerning you, but He who sent Me is true; and the things which I heard from Him, these I speak to the world." They did not realize that He had been speaking to them about the Father. So Jesus said, "When you lift up the Son of Man, then you will know that I am He, and I do nothing on My own initiative, but I speak these things as the Father taught Me. And He who sent Me is with Me; He has not left Me alone, for I always do the things that are pleasing to Him" (John 8:26-29 NASB).

For I did not speak on My own initiative, but the Father Himself who sent Me has given Me a commandment as to what to say (John 12:49-50 NASB).

Do you not believe that I am in the Father, and the Father is in Me? The words that I say to you I do not speak on My own initiative, but the Father abiding in Me does His works (John 14:10 NASB).

I want to bring into this line of thought something that is revealed in the Greek language in Matthew 16:18-19 and again in Matthew 18:18. The Amplified Bible, the *Concordant Literal*

New Testament, The Greek Testament Englished: Annotated, and *The Passion Translation,* as well as other translations, indicate that binding and loosing must *first* take place in Heaven, and then it can effectively be done in earth.

The Greek word for *bind* means to forbid, prohibit, declare to be illicit. The Greek word for *loose* means to declare lawful. From the nature of the action this is something that has to do with carrying out a verdict or judgment rendered from a court action. Therefore, to attempt to do this independent of the leading of the Holy Spirit would essentially carry no real authority in the realm of the spirit.

Additionally, this was not given to Peter exclusively, but to the Ecclesia, the governmental Body of Christ that Jesus indicated in John 15:4-5 can do nothing apart from Him. The authority of the Body of Christ is *delegated* authority, but in this instance *delegated* must be understood to be granted to function within the same constraints that Jesus Himself functioned in authority while in the earth. He did nothing and said nothing of His own initiative.

I am highlighting this point due to its importance for our success in the Kingdom of God. And to show this is another perspective, let's go to Matthew chapter 7, and read the words of Jesus in verses 21 through 23.

> *Not everyone who says to Me, "Lord, Lord," shall enter the kingdom of heaven, but he who does the will of My Father in heaven. Many will say to Me in that day, "Lord, Lord, have we not prophesied in Your name, cast out demons in Your name, and done many*

wonders in Your name?" And then I will declare to them, "I never knew you; depart from Me, you who practice lawlessness!"

Lawlessness is another way of describing iniquity. Self-willed actions, no matter how well intended, are a form of lawlessness and iniquity. Judges 17:6 speaks of a time when the nation of Israel had a problem with self-will and describes it this way: *"In those days there was no king in Israel; everyone did what was right in his own eyes."*

The Body of Christ has a King, who is also the head, and we must receive our instructions from Him and refrain from self-willed words and actions. As Romans 8:14 declares, *"For as many as are led by the Spirit of God, these are sons of God."*

To be led means we are responding to the impulse, influence, and guidance of the Holy Spirit in exactly the same way that Jesus did when He lived upon this earth. This means we do *only* what the head of the Body shows us to do; we say *only* what the head of the Body tells us to say. To do otherwise is to commit iniquity or to live lawlessly. And when we do choose to go our own way, even in doing good things, we open the door for the adversary to have legal accusations against us and to build legal cases against us.

Many times this propensity to be self-willed is connected to iniquities in our bloodline that energizes stubbornness, willfulness, and lawlessness in our lives. There are any number of characteristics that can be seen in family behavior and characteristics that reflect this iniquitous propensity that is generational in its origins. It has roots that need to be removed by cleansing the bloodline through the Courts of Heaven to break the back of the adversary's legal right to keep these mind-sets and behaviors in the family one generation to the next.

Any one of the dimensions of satanic characteristics, or multiple characteristics, can be iniquitous infections that are used by the adversary to delay, hinder, and deny Christians their God-designed destinies, but can be used against the callings and destinies of entire family lines. Let's look at some of examples.

When the prophet Samuel grew old and set his sons over Israel as judges, things began to shift in a direction that was not good. His sons did not live in the same manner as Samuel, and they began to be turned by the love of money, taking bribes and perverting judgment. Samuel did not deal with this iniquity, and it led to the leaders of Israel meeting with Samuel and make a request for a king to rule the nation.

Samuel knew this was not right. So we see in First Samuel 8 something very interesting in the conversation between God and Samuel concerning this situation.

> But the thing displeased Samuel when they said, "Give us a king to judge us." So Samuel prayed to the Lord. And the Lord said to Samuel, "Heed the voice of the people in all that they say to you; for they have not rejected you, but they have rejected Me, that I should not reign over them. According to all the works which they have done since the day that I brought them up out of Egypt, even to this day—with which they have

*forsaken Me and served other gods—so they are doing
to you also. Now therefore, heed their voice. However,
you shall solemnly forewarn them, and show them
the behavior of the king who will reign over them"*
(vv. 6-9).

We can see that the problem with Israel was self-will, iniquity. And God saw that their self-willed desire to be like all the other nations and have a king to rule over them was not going to be able to be dealt with, so He gave them what they stubbornly wanted. This set up a chain of events that were all fueled by the adversary having a legal case against the entire nation, and it set them up to have a king that had an iniquitous heart and not a heart after God.

After Samuel anointed Saul as king of Israel, he gave him certain instructions, one of which would be a critical test of Saul's obedience. This is found in First Samuel 10:8.

*You shall go down before me to Gilgal; and surely I
will come down to you to offer burnt offerings and
make sacrifices of peace offerings. Seven days you shall
wait, till I come to you and show you what you should
do.*

Saul went on to Gilgal, and while there he attacked the Philistines, which prompted a greater attack by the Philistines in response. As the Philistine army was gathering against Israel, the people began to disperse and hide; and even some of the Israelite soldiers began to flee. We pick up this story in

First Samuel 13 beginning midway through verse 7 and going through verse 14.

> *As for Saul, he was still in Gilgal, and all the people followed him trembling. Then he waited seven days, according to the time set by Samuel. But Samuel did not come to Gilgal; and the people were scattered from him. So Saul said, "Bring a burnt offering and peace offerings here to me." And he offered the burnt offering. Now it happened, as soon as he had finished presenting the burnt offering, that Samuel came; and Saul went out to meet him, that he might greet him. And Samuel said, "What have you done?" Saul said, "When I saw that the people were scattered from me, and that you did not come within the days appointed, and that the Philistines gathered together at Michmash, then I said, 'The Philistines will now come down on me at Gilgal, and I have not made supplication to the Lord.' Therefore I felt compelled, and offered a burnt offering." And Samuel said to Saul, "You have done foolishly. You have not kept the commandment of the Lord your God, which He commanded you. For now the Lord would have established your kingdom over Israel forever. But now your kingdom shall not continue. The Lord has sought for Himself a man after His own heart, and the Lord has commanded him to be commander over His people, because you have not kept what the Lord commanded you."*

Saul's self-willed actions cost his family from being the royal family over Israel. Iniquity disqualified any of Saul's heritage from ever sitting on the throne of Israel. But Saul was not through demonstrating his iniquitous ways.

In First Samuel 15 we find the Lord giving King Saul another assignment through the prophet Samuel. He was to attack and completely destroy the Amalekites for they were stark enemies of Israel. They were so dangerous to Israel's future that God wanted Saul to destroy the king and all the people, even down to the infants and animals (see 1 Sam. 15:1-3).

But Saul disobeyed the Lord. In verses 8 and 9 it explains that Saul saved King Agag and spared the best of the sheep, oxen, and other animals that could be used as a sacrifice. This prompted an immediate response from the Lord to Samuel, explaining to Samuel that Saul was now rejected as king of Israel because of his disobedience.

You can read this complete story in First Samuel 15, but I will share here the key verses that reveal the iniquitous heart of Saul, when confronted over his disobedience. This is found in verses 20 through 23.

> *And Saul said to Samuel, "But I have obeyed the voice of the Lord, and gone on the mission on which the Lord sent me, and brought back Agag king of Amalek; I have utterly destroyed the Amalekites. But the people took of the plunder, sheep and oxen, the best of the things which should have been utterly destroyed, to sacrifice to the Lord your God in Gilgal."*

So Samuel said: "Has the Lord as great delight in burnt offerings and sacrifices, as in obeying the voice of the Lord? Behold, to obey is better than sacrifice, and to heed than the fat of rams. For rebellion is as the sin of witchcraft, and stubbornness is as iniquity and idolatry. Because you have rejected the word of the Lord, He also has rejected you from being king."

This cost Saul the throne immediately. Iniquity cost both he and his family the right to rule Israel. It also led to a series of iniquitous acts by Saul as he continued to demonstrate his rebellion before the Lord, and it cost him and much of his family their lives. The adversary had the legal right to do this, taking the life of even Jonathan who actually had a heart toward God and had entered into blood covenant with David, the one who replaced Saul as king. There is so much more we could glean from this, but I want to share one other similar situation when iniquity ended up destroying an entire royal family.

In First Kings 12 through 14 we find the story of Jeroboam, who was of the tribe of Ephraim, and the son of a leprous widow. He had worked for King Solomon, but later began to have his heart turned against Solomon. A prophet named Ahijah came to Jeroboam and prophesied to him. The essence of this prophecy was that God was removing the kingdom of Israel out of Solomon's hand and ten tribes would be taken and Jeroboam would be made king over them. The other two tribes would remain in the house of David to be ruled by his sons (see 1 Kings 11).

The promise from God to Jeroboam was that his house would remain on the throne of Israel as long as he followed the Lord. This was not to be though.

Jeroboam began to commit sins and atrocities that were very egregious. Idolatry began to be fostered by Jeroboam, and he even made himself one of the priests of the high places where the idolatrous worship took place (see 1 Kings 13).

We see in First Kings 13:33-34 that this iniquity became the legal thing that gave the adversary the right to totally destroy Jeroboam and his family.

> *Jeroboam did not turn from his evil way, but again he made priests from every class of people for the high places; whoever wished, he consecrated him, and he became one of the priests of the high places. And this thing was the sin of the house of Jeroboam, so as to exterminate and destroy it from the face of the earth.*

The adversary will use iniquity to legally go after families, especially those who present a real governmental threat to his evil plans and purposes. When he uses these legal matters as the basis of his strategies, spiritual warfare will not be able to keep everything that the enemy is using against that family from taking place. The only place to secure total deliverance will be the Courts of Heaven, where the legal rights can be removed.

One aspect of iniquity that has not been understood is that there comes a time that iniquity reaches a point at which the very accumulation of its affects calls for judgment when repentance is not made. Jesus made this clear when He addressed the Pharisees and religious leaders of His day. Look at this passage from Matthew 23:27-38.

> *Woe to you, scribes and Pharisees, hypocrites! For you are like whitewashed tombs which indeed appear beautiful outwardly, but inside are full of dead men's bones and all uncleanness. Even so you also outwardly appear righteous to men, **but inside you are full of hypocrisy and lawlessness.** Woe to you, scribes and Pharisees, hypocrites! Because you build the tombs of the prophets and adorn the monuments of the righteous, and say, "If we had lived in the days of our fathers, we would not have been partakers with them in the blood of the prophets."*
>
> *Therefore you are witnesses against yourselves that you are sons of those who murdered the prophets. Fill up, then, the measure of your fathers' guilt. Serpents, brood of vipers! How can you escape the condemnation of hell? Therefore, indeed, I send you prophets, wise men, and scribes: some of them you will kill and crucify, and some of them you will scourge in your synagogues and persecute from city to city, that on you may come all the righteous blood shed on the earth, from the blood of righteous Abel to the blood of Zechariah, son of Berechiah, whom you murdered between the temple and the altar. Assuredly, I say to you, all these things will come upon this generation.*

O Jerusalem, Jerusalem, the one who kills the proph-
ets and stones those who are sent to her! How often
I wanted to gather your children together, as a hen
gathers her chicks under her wings, but you were not
willing! See! Your house is left to you desolate.

You can see from my emphasized portions of this passage that Jesus made it very clear that the iniquity of previous generations who had killed the prophets and righteous people had been building up. And we see that Jesus was indicating that the present generation of religious leaders were filling up the measure of iniquity, and that would lead to judgment.

Genesis 15:16 speaks of how the iniquity of the Amorites had not yet reached that point of fullness. Iniquity is a different breed of sin, for it has its roots all the way back to when lucifer, through self-will, defiled himself and was cast out of Heaven as a result.

One very important point that needs to be made is with respect to what could be called a "statute of limitations" on iniquity as far as its legal implications can go from one generation to the next. These passages show how far iniquity can be legally used against us by the adversary.

Thou shalt not bow down thyself to them, nor serve
them: for I the Lord thy God am a jealous God, visit-
ing the iniquity of the fathers upon the children unto
the third and fourth generation of them that hate me
(Exodus 20:5 KJV).

Keeping mercy for thousands, forgiving iniquity and transgression and sin, and that will by no means clear the guilty; visiting the iniquity of the fathers upon the children, and upon the children's children, unto the third and to the fourth generation (Exodus 34:7 KJV).

The Lord is longsuffering, and of great mercy, forgiving iniquity and transgression, and by no means clearing the guilty, visiting the iniquity of the fathers upon the children unto the third and fourth generation (Numbers 14:18 KJV).

Thou shalt not bow down thyself unto them, nor serve them: for I the Lord thy God am a jealous God, visiting the iniquity of the fathers upon the children unto the third and fourth generation of them that hate me (Deuteronomy 5:9 KJV).

This imposition of a statute of limitations on iniquity is imposed by God Himself. The adversary does not have the right to search out iniquity going all the way back to Adam, even though the infection of sin goes back that far according to what we have already learned in Acts 17:26 and Romans 5:12. We can see how God only counted three generations to establish the covenant line of blessing; Abraham, Isaac, and Jacob. And, the apostle Paul counted the generational inheritance of faith in Timothy's family three generations (see 2 Tim. 1:5).

This doesn't mean that iniquity does not exist beyond the fourth generation; it just means that the adversary cannot use iniquity as a legal means past that point. We actually can use this to our advantage when dealing with the legal issues that may be needing to be removed out of the way in the Court of Heaven.

I keep repeating this, but this must be understood: the adversary using iniquity as a legal means to delay, hinder, and deny a believer from receiving any aspect of their rightful inheritance is not due to God remembering sin or iniquity! It is that our physical bodies have not yet experienced redemption. The iniquity of the bloodline gives the enemy the right to tempt us in the area of fleshly passion; it's our propensity to sin that has given him that right through generational yielding.

The finished work of redemption, through which we received the new birth, opened the door to the Courts of Heaven by making us priests of the heavenly order of Melchizedek. That priesthood is granted authority in the Courts of Heaven to deal with any issues that have to do with our inheritance, including attempts to legally hinder our rights and privileges as joint heirs with Christ and heirs of God. Jesus, as the Righteous Judge, and God, our heavenly Father, have empowered the courts to deal with every legal matter that pertains to our earthly walk and authority where dealing with the enemy is concerned.

As we learn to utilize the Courts of Heaven and walk in a greater dimension of our sonship, we will find that our ability to deal with the devil's attacks become much more effective because we are approaching him from a legal perspective, even when we face him in a battlefield situation. The whole strategy of the Kingdom of God where our functioning from our heavenly seating is concerned is based upon the absolute spiritual law that we can do nothing independent of our living union with Christ. It is our protection from self-will, which we have learned is iniquity.

The understanding that there is a statute of limitations on how far back the adversary can search out our bloodline is also unveiled in two New Testament scriptures. First Timothy 1:3-4 speaks of avoiding the issue of endless genealogies.

> *As I urged you when I left for Macedonia, I'm asking that you remain in Ephesus to instruct them not to teach or follow the error of deceptive doctrines, nor pay any attention to cultural myths, traditions, or the endless study of genealogies. Those digressions only breed controversies and debates. They are devoid of power that builds up and strengthens the church in the faith of God* (TPT).

This same instruction is found in Titus 3:9, "*But avoid useless controversies, genealogies, pointless quarrels, and arguments over the law, which will get you nowhere*" (TPT). Even with the potential of the adversary using something in our bloodline as a legal means to stop us, we must not make the aspect of genealogy our focus. Our focus is securing our legal right through the blood of Jesus to answer every legal accusation the adversary may attempt to use against us.

Chapter 9

MY STORY OF FREEDOM FROM INIQUITY

There are a couple of passages from the New Testament that I want to present at the beginning of my story that have great meaning to me, even greater than ever before because I am enjoying the manifestation of what these passages are speaking about in my life. My freedom and liberty is not "by faith" at this point; it is real, substantive, and my daily experience.

John 8:31-32,36 is where I will begin.

> *Then Jesus said to those Jews who believed Him, "If you abide in My word, you are My disciples indeed. And you shall know the truth, and the truth shall make you free." Therefore if the Son makes you free, you shall be free indeed.*

I will share a quote of a note on verse 32 from *The Passion Translation* that Dr. Brian Simmons wrote to give greater understanding of what Jesus was speaking about. "The truth Jesus gives us releases us from the bondage of our past, the bondage of our sins, and the bondage of religion. Jesus is speaking these words to those who were not fully free from man's traditions. Truth must be embraced and worked out through the divine process of spiritual maturity. The Greek word for 'truth' is *reality*. To embrace the reality of Christ brings more freedom into your life."[19]

I will use an illustration to depict what is being explained here in the light of what actually happens when we get born again. Image someone who has been locked up in a prison for most of their life. All they have known is the restricted and confined life within the prison. Then one day someone comes and secures their release and unlocks the prison door to their cell and tells them, "You are now free!"

Suddenly, the life they have known for years is over. There is nothing they need to do but leave. So, they take the necessary steps to leave the cell, walk out of that prison, and step into a new life with no limitations and boundaries. They are liberated and free!

There is a problem though. This newly liberated person is no longer a prisoner, but they are wearing prison clothes, they have a prisoner's mentality, they speak the language of the prison lifestyle, and they have all the habits they learned while in prison. And one other thing is true—they come from a family of criminals. They are free from a geographical perspective, but everything else about them has them connected to criminal activity and the resulting prison sentence and lifestyle.

For this person to remain free and actually begin to experience true freedom in their daily life, they will have to begin to get rid of all the connections to the old life and begin to install elements of the new life on every level of speaking, thinking, and behaving. They will have to embrace the lifestyle that will keep them free. Old thinking will lead right back to prison.

This person has been set free, but now they must be *made* free. The difference is that having been set free, the potential exists that they may end up back in prison. However, if they are made free, they are free in a very real, organic, and substantive way. They are free not just geographically in the sense that their address is no longer the prison, but they also have absolutely no evidence in their words, thinking, or behavior that they were ever in prison. This is what Jesus was describing, and this is what true Christianity offers. However, it is not automatic!

I found out a few years ago that the word *religion* means "obligation, bond."[20] The Latin word *religiō*, possibly derived from the verb *regliāre*, "tie back, tie tight."[21]

It has to be understood that Christianity is not a religion! It is a living union with Jesus Christ through the power and presence of the Holy Spirit that comes into being by being re-fathered from God, who is the Father of all spirits! (See Hebrews 12:9.)

James 1:21-26 is another passage that is important to my story.

> *Therefore lay aside all filthiness and overflow of wickedness, and receive with meekness the implanted word, which is able to save your souls. But be doers of the word, and not hearers only, deceiving yourselves. For if anyone is a hearer of the word and not a doer, he is like a man observing his natural face in a mirror; for he observes himself, goes away, and immediately forgets what kind of man he was. But he who looks into the perfect law of liberty and continues in it, and is not a forgetful hearer but a doer of the work, this one will be blessed in what he does. If anyone among you thinks he is religious, and does not bridle his tongue but deceives his own heart, this one's religion is useless.*

When I received the new birth on the day I gave my life to Jesus, Sunday, February 13, 1977, I was let out of prison. I received the baptism of the Holy Spirit and began immediately to speak in that wonderful heavenly language that empowered my prayer life in a way that was indescribable! Things were new, fresh, and exciting! However, I was not completely free; I had work to do to build the reality of what had taken place in my spirit into my mind, and I needed to learn new habits. Habits are learned through discipline and training. I needed to renew my mind and exercise dominion over my physical body. This, as I learned with much frustration, would be a lifelong process of growth and maturity.

From an early age, about two years old, I had a very real problem with extreme anger. My parents described my behavior as beginning as young as when a toddler. I would get so mad that I would literally get down on my hands and knees and beat my head on the floor until I bruised my forehead. This violent display of anger continued as I grew older, although it gradually shifted into other displays of angry behavior.

In my teen years and on into my twenties, prior to receiving Jesus as my Lord, I would explode in anger and became quite prolific with the use of cuss words. I would create new cuss words, many times various combinations of foul and putrid words that were demonically inspired would flow like a river under the force of my out-of-control temper.

After I was born again, the foul language abated, for the most part, but the anger continued to be an issue. I married my wife, Lorie, in January of 1982. I had already begun to take ministry assignments as early as 1980. The anger was still a major area of challenge for me, even though I knew it needed to stop, and I did all I knew to try and control it, but to no avail.

Lorie and I pioneered a church in 1984, and it began to grow and flourish. But the anger continued. One day, sometime in 1986, I blew up over some kind of disagreement with Lorie, went into a verbal rage, and came to myself on the floor of the closet in our bedroom, crying out to God for help. I knew that if I didn't get a handle on the anger , it would destroy my marriage and my ministry.

The Holy Spirit began to lead me to meditate and confess Scriptures that dealt with anger and controlling it. Little by little I gained more control over the outbursts. However, while there was progress, if I got spiritually lazy or overly tired, I would find myself succumbing to the pressure that fueled the anger.

This off and on again battle continued until after I began to learn about the Courts of Heaven toward the end of 2016 and throughout 2017. During the summer of 2017, the Lord spoke to me and told me to bring my anger issue to the Courts of Heaven.

I had learned that both of my parents had been raised in homes where anger was directed toward them on many occasions. Doing some investigating of both my mother's and my father's backgrounds, I saw that there was a definite generational iniquity of anger in both their bloodlines.

To add to the strength of the anger issues, on my dad's side of the family, he and his mother had been abandoned by my dad's father when my dad was around five years of age. This definitely had an adverse effect on my dad. That plus the reality that in his adolescent years his mom's parents would slap or beat him when he was living in their home added to the culture of anger that he knew growing up.

There were frequent arguments, some quite heated, between my mom and dad that I observed or heard when I was growing up. In reflecting on all of this, I realized that the bloodline iniquity of anger had taken root in my parents and the mind-set that supported uncontrolled anger was part of my inheritance. Now, as a grown adult in my early sixties I was discovering that I had been programmed with a predisposition for anger, and the devil made sure that anger was energized in my life at a very early age.

Another issue was that although both of my parents were Christians, and my mother was recognized as a powerful Bible teacher, they did not have any understanding or revelation of what was behind the anger they fought or was evident in my life from the age of two.

Iniquity in the bloodline will shape your identity and cause you to accept things that you should never accept. When you fight and fight something with little or no results, the reality of deferred hope kicks in and you resign yourself to a fate that is not of God's design. This is one of the dangers of iniquity.

For just a moment I want to illustrate this point by taking you to Isaiah 6. Let's read verses 1 through 8.

> *In the year that King Uzziah died, I saw the Lord sitting on a throne, high and lifted up, and the train of His robe filled the temple. Above it stood seraphim; each one had six wings: with two he covered his face, with two he covered his feet, and with two he flew. And one cried to another and said: "Holy, holy, holy is the Lord of hosts; the whole earth is full of His glory!" And the posts of the door were shaken by the voice of him who cried out, and the house was filled with smoke. So I said: "Woe is me, for I am undone! Because I am a man of unclean lips, and I dwell in the midst*

of a people of unclean lips; for my eyes have seen the King, the Lord of hosts."

Then one of the seraphim flew to me, having in his hand a live coal which he had taken with the tongs from the altar. And he touched my mouth with it, and said: "Behold, this has touched your lips; your iniquity is taken away, and your sin purged."

Also I heard the voice of the Lord, saying: "Whom shall I send, and who will go for Us?" Then I said, "Here am I! Send me."

Isaiah saw a vision of the Lord as He sat upon His throne. The impact of seeing the Lord in all His glory and hearing and seeing the angelic activity around the throne caused Isaiah to become aware of how much of a sinner and how unholy he actually was.

As he cried out of this awareness of uncleanness, one of the angels (a seraphim) took a live coal off the altar in the throne room (which is where the Court of Heaven is located) and touched Isaiah's mouth with the live coal.

The angel explained that by doing that, Isaiah's iniquity had been removed and his sin purged. This would have been before the blood of Jesus had been brought into the heavenly holy of holies, so the fire of the altar before the throne was used to deal with the iniquity.

Immediately, Isaiah hears the Lord asking a question concerning a mission that was needing to be fulfilled in the earth. Isaiah immediately responded to this question and volunteered for the assignment. With the iniquity purged, Isaiah gained a new perspective of his identity and no longer saw himself as unclean and unworthy, but ready and able to do the Lord's bidding. The iniquity had shaped Isaiah's identity and warped his understanding of his destiny. With it removed, he could move forward in confidence, knowing that he was able to do something that moments before he was unable to image anything but his unworthiness.

The iniquity of anger had certainly contributed to my inability to comprehend the fullness of all that God had called me to accomplish. On many occasions I felt that I was either unworthy or disqualified to step into the greater dimensions that God might have for me to do, all because iniquity had blinded my eyes to my own potential.

One afternoon, after the Lord spoke to me to come to the court to deal with the anger, I did just that. By faith I stepped before the Lord as the Righteous Judge, and I acknowledged the iniquity of anger in my bloodlines of both parents. I repented of the anger and asked that the blood of Jesus would speak on my behalf to remove and remit the iniquity of anger out of my life, my bloodline, and my children's life. As did that, I stood on Colossians 2:14:

> *He canceled out every legal violation we had on our record and the old arrest warrant that stood to indict us. He erased it all—our sins, our stained soul—he deleted it all and they cannot be retrieved! Everything we once were in Adam has been placed onto his cross and nailed permanently there as a public display of cancellation* (TPT).

This was actually executing into place the verdict of the cross and applying the judgment of the cross against the legal claim that the adversary had been holding in place to have a legal right to keep energizing that iniquity of anger that was in the bloodline of my family. The whole process took about fifteen minutes.

I sensed something had changed; I was aware that I had broken the back of that anger, once and for all! But the confirmation of that came a couple weeks later when I happened to have an opportunity to have dinner with my son, Grant.

While he and I were having dinner together, the Lord told me to share with him what I had done in taking the anger issue to the Court of Heaven. So, I did. Grant listened intently to my story, and when I was through, he asked me when that took place. I told him that it had been two weeks.

Grant responded that it was at that same time that all the anger left him! He said that he woke up every morning mad at the world and really couldn't understand why. He also had to deal with an extremely short fuse with his anger, and he would go into a blinding rage with little or no provocation. What I also knew was that when he was a toddler, he had displayed the same behavior I had displayed, beating his head on the floor. Lorie had taken authority over it, and he only did it one time, but the anger was still there and had plagued Grant for all those years.

So, not only was I free from the influence of that bloodline iniquity, so was my son! There is an important distinction that I want to make here. Only by staying strong in the Word and faith was I able to "control" the impulses of anger. I wasn't truly free from it, but I kept it under control. However, if I ever let up in the Word or got tired mentally and physically, I was subject to having to fight that iniquitous pressure; many times it would get the best of me. By going to the Court of Heaven I was able to remove the iniquity from my bloodline, which not only made me free, but also freed my children from the legal aspects of that iniquity as well.

There have been other similar addictive behaviors that I have completely removed from my bloodline, and by so doing, I have become completely free from the temptation of those things, and at the same time removed the legal right of the adversary to tempt my children and grandchildren with those same issues.

I have found permanent deliverance from several longtime afflictions and behavioral patterns that had not responded to years of applying the principles of faith and prayer. I want to emphasize that I am no novice to the faith message or lifestyle. I have seen and received major victories in my life and ministry over the years that came as a result of applying the principles of faith and prayer that my mentors in the faith have taught, going back to the late 1970s. I cut my spiritual teeth on subjects like the authority of the believer, the power of the name of Jesus, in Christ realities, and so many other subjects that are well beyond the elementary subjects handled in Sunday school quarterlies.

So when I hear the question asked in a push-back against the revelation of the Courts of Heaven like, "Why didn't you just take authority over the anger, resist the devil, and be done with it?" My answer is, "I did!" But with little or no results. One might say, "Well, you must have not had enough faith to deal with it!" My answer is that sometimes "having enough faith" is not enough to see a breakthrough or get permanent victory. It can boil down to how you are applying your faith or not having enough knowledge of what dimension faith needs to be released in or directed. It could also be that something legal was allowing the anger to resist all efforts to remove it.

This brings me to a point that needs to be addressed. I have been in this ministry for forty years at this point. As I stated at the beginning of this book, there have been a number of people who were strong in faith who have lost their lives to terminal disease in very recent times (something far more serious than dealing with anger). In fact, I was sharing with a major leader in the Body of Christ recently that the casualty rate in the Body of Christ, especially in the ranks of those who believe in healing and have been taught and have been teaching faith for decades, is unacceptable.

The particularly troubling situation was when the person who died was a person of strong faith, part of a church known for teaching a message of faith and healing, received prayer from people who were seasoned prayer warriors who knew how to pray and understood how to deal with devilish attacks, yet the curse was not turned away.

These were not battles that were fought half-heartedly, nor were the people involved living compromised lives. Something was keeping the prayers and stand of faith from being successful.

Something other than a battlefield tactic that had never been faced before was keeping the curse from responding to faith, authority, and anointing. There was something legal that was resisting the attempts to secure healing and deliverance. And no one knew to, or how, to go into the Courts of Heaven and find out what the legal issue was and how to address it to remove it. This is fixable!

Not everything is a battlefield issue. And sickness and disease doesn't have the right to stand in the face of an onslaught of faith and authority in the name of Jesus. There just might be a need to add some additional tools to our arsenal that will help us get results when we recognize that time is being used against us as a weapon. The Courts of Heaven and our learning how to function in our heavenly seat and priesthood is at least one additional tool that we need to learn to answer situations that are not quickly responding to our prayers of faith and authority.

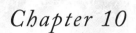

Chapter 10

PROBATING THE NEW TESTAMENT INHERITANCE

Jesus Christ is the only man who has written a will, died to put the will into effect, and then was raised from the dead to probate His own will! His will is recorded in the pages of what we know as the New Testament, particularly the letters of the apostles: Paul, James, Jude Peter, and John. In those letters we find what our rights and privileges are as new creation citizens of Heaven.

Romans 8:16-17 reveals that we are joint heirs with Christ: *"The Spirit Himself bears witness with our spirit that we are children of God, and if children, then heirs—heirs of God and joint heirs with Christ."* As joint heirs with Christ we are equal heirs; this is not a fifty/fifty proposition, but one hundred/one hundred. In other words, if Christ owns it, we own it; if we own it, Christ owns it.

The ultimate possession identified throughout the Bible that is Christ's inheritance is found specifically in Psalm 2:8, *"Ask of Me, and I will give You the nations for Your inheritance, and the ends of the earth for Your possession."* It is this very inheritance, lost to the devil by Adam's iniquity, that satan used to tempt Jesus at the beginning of His earthly ministry. Read this in Luke 4:5-8.

> *Then the devil, taking Him up on a high moun-*
> *tain, showed Him all the kingdoms of the world in*
> *a moment of time. And the devil said to Him, "All*
> *this authority I will give You, and their glory; for this*
> *has been delivered to me, and I give it to whomever*
> *I wish. Therefore, if You will worship before me, all*
> *will be Yours." And Jesus answered and said to him,*
> *"Get behind Me, Satan! For it is written, 'You shall*
> *worship the Lord your God, and Him only you shall*
> *serve.'"*

The devil was not lying about possessing all the nations and wealth; Adam had turned all of that over to satan when he sinned in the Garden of Eden. The lie was that satan would give all the authority to Jesus if He would worship the devil; that was an out and out lie. Jesus knew it; He knew that because of what He was ultimately sent to do, He would receive all of that as His inheritance.

Colossians 2:15 states that when Jesus was raised from the dead, He made an open show of satan and his demonic hordes, triumphing over them all and spoiling them. The New Testament declares that Jesus was exalted to the right hand of God, seated far above all other beings, powers, and dominions, and given a name that is above every other name (see Eph. 1:19-23; Phil. 2:9-11; Heb. 1:3).

We also know that Hebrews 2:14-15 describes that Jesus "destroyed" the one who once possessed the power of death, which is the devil.

> *Inasmuch then as the children have partaken of flesh and blood, He Himself likewise shared in the same, that through death He might destroy him who had the power of death, that is, the devil, and release those who through fear of death were all their lifetime subject to bondage.*

Here we have to come to the realization that our modern-day concept of the word *destroy* bears no resemblance to the word as used in verse 14. And as a result, an entire doctrine about the state of the devil after the cross has set God's people up for disappointment. The modern-day usage of *destroy* is "to ruin; to bring to naught; in general, to put an end to; to annihilate a thing or the form in which it exists."[22]

But this is not even close to what the word as used in the Greek means. The Greek word used in Hebrews 2:14 is *katargeō* and literally means "to reduce to inactivity."[23]

W. E. Vine goes on to apply this meaning as used in Hebrews 2:14, "the Devil is to be reduced to inactivity through the death of Christ."[24]

As a second witness to the validity of this definition I will quote from Kenneth S. Wuest's and his explanation of this word as used in Hebrews 2:14 specifically.

> The word "destroy" is the translation of "kater-gazomai," which means "to bring to naught, to render inoperative." Satan was not annihilated at the Cross. His power was broken. Spiritual death cannot hold the person who puts his faith in the Saviour. Physical death cannot keep his body in the grave. The resurrection of the Lord Jesus provides the believer with eternal life, and his body with glorification at the Rapture. Thus, Jesus conquered death, and brought to naught the devil. Satan had the power of death, not in the sense that he had power over death, but that he had the sovereignty of dominion of death. He had a sovereignty of which death is the realm. The word for "power" in the Greek text here is "kratos," which means "power in the sense of dominion." His dominion over the human race was in the form of death. That dominion is now broken.[25]

What this means is that the devil's power to keep any man, woman, or child locked in a state of spiritual death has been broken, and he is powerless to stop them from being born again if they make the decision to receive Jesus as Lord. The devil has been brought to a place of inactivity where keeping people in spiritual death is concerned.

Another passage that is important to our understanding in found in First John 3:8: *"He who sins is of the devil, for the devil has sinned from the beginning. For this purpose the Son of God was manifested, that He might destroy the works of the devil."* Jesus came with a specific purpose: to destroy the works of the devil.

The word *destroy* as used in this verse is from the Greek word *lyō* and has many different meanings based upon the context. One definition is "metaphorically, to overthrow, do away with."[26]

Jesus was manifested to overthrow and do away with the works of the devil. *Works* in this context is liken unto the product or results of employment. In the context of this verse that would be sickness, disease, bondages of all kinds; essentially the manifestation of the curse that entered humanity's life experience as a result of Adam's fall.

Jesus is still doing that, and His primary instrument through which He is accomplishing this purpose is the Body of Christ in the earth. The Church as the governmental Body of people called out of the world and representing and functioning in the Kingdom of God, also known as the Ecclesia, are the ones Jesus has authorized and given delegated authority to deal with every "work" of the devil today. This exercise of Kingdom authority is one of the first demonstrations of the resurrected Lord that is to result in the reclamation and reformation of mankind back to the purposes of God.

In order to fully accomplish this assignment, we, the Ecclesia, have been made both kings and priests so that we may take full advantage of the Finished Work of the Cross of Jesus to see the purposes of God fully realized in our lives individually and around the world in every nation, tribe, and tongue.

At this point in our understanding, I want to show the true nature of our responsibilities as new creation citizens of Heaven, assigned to carry out Kingdom purposes in the earth. This is vastly important to understand because it will pull back the veil that tends to hide the nature of the opposition the true believers in Jesus Christ face in our day and show us how to take advantage of all that Jesus accomplished for us in dealing with satanic strategies to keep demonic powers in a place of influence in this world.

We know, based upon what the apostle Paul writes in Ephesians 1:19-23, that Jesus has taken His place at the right hand of God in Heaven.

> *...and what is the exceeding greatness of His power toward us who believe, according to the working of His mighty power which He worked in Christ when He raised Him from the dead and seated Him at His right hand in the heavenly places, far above all principality and power and might and dominion, and every name that is named, not only in this age but also in that which is to come. And He put all things under His feet, and gave Him to be head over all things to the church, which is His body, the fullness of Him who fills all in all.*

I want to focus on verses 22 and 23 for a moment. Notice that this says that God put all things under Jesus's feet and that the Church is His Body. Take note of Ephesians 2:6: "*...and raised us up together, and made us sit together in the heavenly places in Christ Jesus.*" So, the born-again believer is a member of Christ's Body and is sitting in the same Heavenly seating as Christ, in the same exalted position as Christ.

However, while this is the spiritual position of every born-again believer, it is evident that few are living a life that fully demonstrates the full expression of that place of authority. Scripture is not silent as to what is the state of things from an earthly experience, and this is where we must align with God's purposes more fully.

Let's look at Hebrews 10:12-13 to gain some light on this issue. Verse 10 begins by speaking of Jesus, and what He did in His death, burial, resurrection, and ascension to the right hand of the Father to function as High Priest after the order of Melchizedek.

> *But this Man, after He had offered one sacrifice for sins forever, sat down at the right hand of God, **from that time waiting till His enemies are made His footstool.***

Look at a companion scripture Acts 2:34-36.

> *For David did not ascend into the heavens, but he says himself: "The Lord said to my Lord, '**Sit at My right hand, till I make Your enemies Your footstool.**'" Therefore let all the house of Israel know*

assuredly that God has made this Jesus, whom you crucified, both Lord and Christ.

I want you to see and understand that Jesus's enemies have yet to become His footstool. He is waiting for this to happen. And the ones who are charged with the responsibility of making that happen are His Body, the Ecclesia, the Church.

An interesting verse in Paul's letter to the church at Rome is found in Romans 16:20. *"And the God of peace will crush Satan under your feet shortly. The grace of our Lord Jesus Christ be with you."* I find this interesting because this statement was made after Jesus had taken His place at the right hand of the Father and completed his finished work of redemption. Is it possible that the unseating of the enemy where this earthly dimension is concerned is something that has to be carried by the activities of the Ecclesia and is not an automatic thing?

Let's look at several other passages that communicate this truth in a slightly different way. We will begin in Hebrews 2:6-8.

> *But one testified in a certain place, saying: "What is man that You are mindful of him, or the son of man that You take care of him? You have made him little lower than the angels; You have crowned him with glory and honor, and set him over the works of Your hands. You have put all things in subjection under his feet." For in that He put all in subjection under him, He left nothing that is not put under him. **But now we do not yet see all things put under him.***

Verses 6 and 7 are a direct quote from Psalm 8, except for one part which needs to be pointed out for consideration. In Psalm 8:4-6 we can read this again.

> *Compared to all this cosmic glory, why would you bother with puny, mortal man or be infatuated with Adam's sons? Yet what honor you have given to men, created only a little lower than Elohim, crowned like kings and queens with glory and magnificence. You have delegated to them mastery over all you have made, making everything subservient to their authority, placing earth itself under the feet of your image-bearers* (TPT).

A vast majority of translations render the word *angels* in verse 5 in the same manner as found in *The Passion Translation*. Elohim is the name of God as Creator. Without quoting directly, I will summarize the most common renderings as reading this way: "you have made him a little lower than God." This is the essence of the majority of the translator's understanding of the Hebrew language in verse 5.

This describes man as created in Genesis 1:26: "*Then God said, 'Let Us make man in Our image, according to Our likeness; let them have dominion over the fish of the sea, over the birds of the air, and over the cattle, over all the earth and over every creeping thing that creeps on the earth.*'"

God spoke these words to actually create man's spirit as He breathed the breath of life into His nostrils. God had already established the way He creates in repeated demonstrations of His creative power through speaking words throughout Genesis 1. It stands to reason that He would not have changed His mode of creating by speaking when it came to the pinnacle of His creative purposes.

Man is a spirit, which possesses a soul, consisting of a mind, emotions, and a will; he lives, while in the earth, in a physical body (see 1 Thess. 5:23). The physical body of man is what gives him the right to be in the earth and exercise dominion over the earth.

As long as man remained in a spiritual union with His Creator, he had the capacity and ability to function in perfect harmony with God as an under-ruler over all creation. Man was designed to be led by God and follow His instructions as to what to do and what to say to accomplish God's purposes in the earth. Man's free will was to be exercised in humble submission to a God who was love Himself (see 1 John 4:8, 16)

The purpose of the tree of the knowledge of good and evil was to provide a way for God to instruct man in the understanding of good and evil without actually experiencing it. The fruit of that tree was under man's responsibility to cultivate, protect, and harvest, and the only restriction installed was "Do not eat of it."

God didn't need the fruit; He desired to feed the fruit to man in times of intimate fellowship and reveal to man the truth of good and evil. This would have resulted in man gaining knowledge through revelation that, in turn, would have enabled man to recognize good and evil and know how to receive and benefit from the good and how to avoid the evil.

The reason this is so important to understand is because the tree was a part of the physical dimension designed by God to train man in the business of spiritual trading and stewardship. It could be said that the tree of the knowledge of good and evil represented the principles of firstfruits and tithing. Natural things that would be marked by man as belonging to God for the purpose of learning how to trade natural things for spiritual purposes. This was training for man to become lucifer's replacement in conducting Kingdom business before the Courts of Heaven.

When Adam sinned, he lost his place of authority, and he lost contact with the spirit dimension. He was now in a state of spiritual death, and he could only receive information through the five physical senses as opposed to receiving revelation from God. He was completely limited to the physical dimension. His ability to rule the physical dimension was lost the moment he was cut off from being able to receive from God spiritually.

This is what Jesus came to "undo" through His work at the cross and what we call the finished work of redemption. Jesus had to break satan's hold over mankind that kept men held in darkness and in the realm of spiritual death. He came to open the door for man to be able to walk out of spiritual death and darkness into spiritual life and light. He came to deliver those who all their lifetime had been held in bondage through fear of death and enable men to know the freedom and liberty that comes by living by faith in God.

He also came to put dominion back into the hands of its rightful, created possessor, which is the race of man that lives in union with God. The only ones capable of properly stewarding that dominion are those who have become new creation beings through union with Christ Jesus. Those new creation beings make up the Ecclesia and have the ability, right, and authority to take back dominion. Through spiritual union with the head of all authority and dominion, Jesus Christ, they have become members of His Body.

Jesus, as the head of the Body of Christ, has been raised up and possesses the fullness of that dominion and authority. However, this is where Hebrews 2:8 comes into play; we read that God has put all things in subjection under His feet. And in that, God put all in subjection under Him; He left nothing that is not put under Him. But now at this present time, we do not yet see all things put under Him. Why? Because the Ecclesia, the Body of Christ, is to accomplish the completion of that mission by executing into place the verdict secured by the head, Jesus Christ, in the earth, as it already is manifested in Heaven. God's will, plan, and purpose, as demonstrated in the exaltation of Christ to God's right hand, is to be fully executed against the powers of darkness through and by the Ecclesia, the recreated, spiritually resurrected, body of believers who are in spiritual oneness with Christ while living in the earth.

I want to slightly paraphrase a portion of the excellent insight shared by John A. MacMillan in his book *The Authority of the Believer*. This selection of his teaching gives some all-important understanding as to what the problem of the modern-day Church is and why we must begin to align ourselves more accurately with God's Kingdom purposes.

> Why, then, is there not more manifest progress? Because [the Head, Jesus Christ], is wholly dependent upon [His Body] for the carrying out of [His] plan. All the members of [His Body] must be subservient, that through their [the Head and the Body] coordinated ministry may be accomplished what is purposed. The Lord Jesus, "Head over all things to the church, which is His body" (Ephesians 1:22-23), is hindered in His mighty plans and working, because His Body has failed to appreciate the deep meaning of His exaltation and to respond to the gracious impulses which He is constantly sending for its quickening.[27]

In other words, self-willed ministry, that is initiated independent of the head, is iniquitous at its root and cannot accomplish what the head desires to see accomplished because it is not according to His will. Add to that the complete lack of responsiveness from those in the Body who would rather live carnal lives more influenced by the world's impulses than those of the indwelling Holy Spirit, and you can see that Jesus's plans and purposes are being frustrated by a completely uncoordinated, and many times, unresponsive Body. This needs to be corrected!

Another dimension of this is when many who claim to be born again refuse to accept or believe in the baptism in the Holy Spirit with the subsequent manifestations of the Spirit that are designed to establish the validity of the message through signs, miracles, and wonders. MacMillan speaks to the purpose of the fullness of the Holy Spirit in this statement from his book. "The fullness of the Spirit is the incoming of the Spirit of God to empower the human spirit for the carrying into effect of the accepted will of the Head."[28]

What we read in Hebrews 2:8 is also found in First Corinthians 15:24-28. This is a very important passage from the New Testament.

> *Then comes the end, when He delivers the kingdom to God the Father, when He puts an end to all rule and all authority and power. For He must reign till He has put all enemies under His feet. The last enemy that will be destroyed is death. For "He has put all things under His feet." But when He says, "all things are put under Him," it is evident that He who put all things under Him is excepted. Now when all things are made subject to Him, then the Son Himself will also be subject to Him who put all things under Him, that God may be all in all.*

When this speaks of Jesus putting to an end all rule and all authority and power, it has to be understood that this includes what Jesus, as the head of the Body, is doing even today through the coordinated work of the Body of Christ, the Ecclesia. It is when we work together with Him and through Him that all rule and all authority and all power is being put down.

To have all His enemies put under His feet, it has to be understood that this is including the Body of Christ, as the feet are in the body and not in the head. When all things are subjected to Him, it is understood that includes being subjected to the Body of Christ as well. The body is one with the head!

That this subjecting is spoken of as a future event, even after the ascension of Christ to the right hand of God, indicates that the work is to be done by Christ through the Body of Christ and not independent of the Body. We, the Body of Christ, are the agents who do the subjecting, with the initiating power and influence of the head energizing our words and actions.

Christ's inheritance has been secured by His work of redemption. But the earthly possessing of that inheritance is being contested by the devil and his demonic hordes. That contest is not just playing out in the context of a spiritual battle unfolding on a battlefield; it also is playing out in the context of a spiritual conflict of a judicial nature as satan, working as both an adversary and accuser, seeks to fight the right to manifest the will of the head in legal maneuvers as well.

This plays out in legal strategies designed to frustrate, hinder, delay, and deny the Body of Christ in the earth from walking in, manifesting, and receiving the full benefits of what Jesus bought and paid for where our joint inheritance is concerned. The outcome of these strategies is focused on physical health, financial and material wealth, relationships, and so many other dimensions of our earthly walk and experience.

As I stated before, an inheritance can be legally contested by a legal opponent; when that happens, nothing is going to take place in the actual transfer of the inheritance until a judgement from the probate court is secured. In the case of a no-show in court by the rightful heir, the opponent can win by virtue of a default judgment. Too many times this is the way things have played out where the Body of Christ is concerned and this needs to stop!

It is imperative that born-again believers begin to take their important role in carrying out the plans and purposes of Jesus Christ in the earth much more seriously than ever before. It is critical that the Body of Christ truly takes its place in the Kingdom of God and enforces the verdict of the finished work of redemption on every level, not just in the realm of spiritual warfare, but also by answering any and all attempts by the enemy functioning as an adversary and accuser in the Courts of Heaven to hinder or stop the rightful possession by Jesus Christ of His inheritance through the agency of the Body of Christ.

Chapter 11

FAITH IS THE VICTORY

I am a product of the Word of Faith message. I have lived and walked by faith for over forty years. I have seen faith produce results in matters that range from small to great. I have received finances, healing in my body, miracle supply for my ministry and church, and so many other wonderful things as a result of faith in God's Word. So, I am experienced in getting results through faith.

One area that I have discovered that I needed to develop and learn to use faith was exposed when I began to attempt to function in the Courts of Heaven. I wasn't experienced in using faith to operate in the unseen realm of the spirit to cooperate with the Holy Spirit from my joint seating with Christ and taking advantage of what is available in Christ where the spiritual dimension is concerned. To be totally honest, my faith was earthbound, and this was limiting my ability and usefulness to Jesus, especially in the role of functioning as a priest in the realm of heavenly matters that had earthly ramifications.

The Holy Spirit began to teach me the absolute necessity of learning to work with Him, as my advocate, and with Jesus, as the Righteous Judge, to secure Kingdom purposes from the realm of Heaven's judicial system. He began to show me from the New Testament how my faith was such a critical part of what Jesus needed to win verdicts, secure judgments, and obtain judicial decrees, which when executed into place in the earth, literally stripped the devil of his power to keep his schemes and strategies working in the earth.

I found out that what the psalmist spoke about in Psalm 84:10 is the absolute truth, *"For a day in Your courts is better than a thousand."* Things that had not responded over years of prayer and confession of the Word were changing, in some instances, in less than twenty-four hours! Granted, there were situations that were so involved in tearing hell's strategies apart they took longer than a day, but it was evident that tapping into the power of the heavenly court system was a game-changing strategy that the devil had no way to defend against.

I discovered that as satisfying as using my faith to receive financial and material things could be, there was nothing compared to learning how to step into the Courts of Heaven by faith and see impossible situations turned around in a much more compressed time frame than I ever thought possible. As a result, I saw that I had grown so accustomed to the idea of "standing and having done all, stand" (Eph. 6:13), I was allowing the devil way too much liberty to jack around in the realm of time and had gotten conditioned to expect battles to last over extended periods of time.

This may have been an acceptable expectation forty years ago, but I was witnessing firsthand that if we didn't learn how to shorten the time frame to get results, we were going to see too many people die unnecessarily; miss opportunities to make impacts in key places around the world; and see the destinies of far too many of God's people be delayed, altered, or even destroyed. I have seen that the Courts of Heaven is the place to go when delay is being implemented as a strategy by the devil.

As I write this, I am thinking about a major ministry that was under severe attack. By working with the leader and teaching him how to take the ministry before the Courts of Heaven, that ministry is no longer threatened. The key to victory was dismantling the legal issues that were giving satan the right to move in and attempt to steal and destroy that ministry.

I am also remembering a dear lady, whose name is Marie, a member of the church I pastor. She watched her mother, who had a strong evangelistic gift, die under the oppression of depression. That same spirit had been attacking Marie, and she had battled it for many years. But regular prayers, confessions of faith, and even ministry from well-known national and international ministers had not been able to permanently remove this demonic depression from this lady.

After a Sunday evening prayer service in November 2016, Marie asked me if I could take her to the Courts of Heaven over this ongoing battle with depression. I had just been introduced to the revelation of the Courts of Heaven through Robert

Henderson's teaching less than a month before. I couldn't have filled a small thimble with what I knew or understood about the courts. But it was obvious that this was a bloodline issue and needed to be stopped. I thought, "How do I do that?" I decided to step out by faith.

In a simple attempt to put what I had heard from Robert's teaching to work, I took Marie before the Courts of Heaven. I presented her case based upon her right to freedom through what Jesus did for her at Calvary. I claimed Colossians 2:14 for her and led her in a simple confession of repentance on behalf of her bloodlines for whatever legal things opened the door to this curse of depression to afflict the family. I ended by thanking Jesus, as the Righteous Judge, for her deliverance. It didn't last even five minutes. At the time I am writing this, two years and four months have passed, and after years of battling depression, Marie has not had a single moment of dealing with depression since that night! Praise God!

Since I grew up in the Word of Faith company, I have heard some of the best teaching and preaching on faith that anyone could be privileged to hear. I can honestly say that even after forty years of studying, teaching, preaching, and living by faith, I am still learning things about faith that are life-changing and powerful.

I want to share a few things that I have learned since coming into the revelation of the Courts of Heaven that has completely revolutionized my life as a believer. My prayer life and my fellowship with the Lord have grown more intense and have borne much greater fruit than anything I have known or understood in a long, long time.

As I share this, I want to establish up front that the foundation to a successful Christian life is knowing and meditating on the written Word of God. God's Word is the basis of faith, and through the Word we are able to gain true revelation of all that is available for the born-again believer through our union with Christ.

The New Testament is the written copy of the promises and governing principles of the blood covenant between Jesus Christ and God, our heavenly Father. Essentially, the record of the sworn oath God made to Jesus upon the presentation of His precious blood in Heaven, when Jesus presented both His blood and Himself as high priest before God after His resurrection, is contained within the pages of what we know as the Letters of the New Testament. Along with the letters, much of what we have recorded in the four Gospels, particularly the Gospel of John, are Jesus's own spoken words revealing important truth that became a part of the New Testament sworn oath.

Faith comes by hearing these words preached, taught, and confessed. Faith is developed through meditation of the Word. Faith is released through words and actions that are given birth to by those same words.

I have also learned that there is a dimension of faith that is absolutely necessary to a life of victory that goes beyond the foundation of the written Word. From that foundation, the Holy Spirit wants to take the born-again believer into a realm of functioning in the Kingdom of God that demands a willingness to step out of a life directed from the outside in and moves to a life directed from the inside out.

The people of great faith listed in Hebrews 11 were obedient to the voice of the Lord. God spoke to them, and they heard His voice. I am convinced that they did not hear God's voice audibly, but what they sensed produced in them a desire to listen and obey that voice. Faith came by hearing; results came by obedience.

The Holy Spirit began to show me some things along this line a couple years ago, and it opened my eyes to see a dimension of God's interaction with people of faith that I had missed for so many years. Read this passage from Second Peter 1:16-21.

> *For we did not follow cunningly devised fables when we made known to you the power and coming of our Lord Jesus Christ, but were eyewitnesses of His majesty. For He received from God the Father honor and glory when such a voice came to Him from the Excellent Glory: "This is My beloved Son, in whom I am well pleased."* ***And we heard this voice which came from heaven when we were with Him on the holy mountain. And so we have the prophetic word confirmed,*** *which you do well to heed as a light that shines in a dark place, until the day dawns and the morning star rises in your hearts; knowing this first, that no prophecy of Scripture is of any private interpretation, for prophecy never came by the will of man,*

but holy men of God spoke as they were moved by the Holy Spirit.

I want you to consider the highlighted portion of this passage, verse 18 and the first part of verse 19: *"And we heard this voice which came from heaven when we were with Him on the holy mountain. And so we have the prophetic word confirmed...."*

Read verses 18 through 21 as translated in *The Passion Translation.*

And we ourselves heard that voice resound from the heavens while we were with him on the holy mountain. And so we have been given the prophetic word—the written message of the prophets, made more reliable and fully validated by the confirming voice of God on the Mount of Transfiguration. And you will continue to do well if you stay focused on it. For this prophetic message is like a piercing light shining in a gloomy place until the dawning of a new day, when the Morning Star rises in your hearts. You must understand this at the outset: Interpretation of scriptural prophecy requires the Holy Spirit, for it does not originate from someone's own imagination. No true prophecy comes from human initiative but is inspired by the moving of the Holy Spirit upon those who spoke the message that came from God.

I could list many other translations of this passage that read exactly the same way. The point being this: the written Word of God at the time that Jesus was on the Mountain of

Transfiguration was the Old Testament. The entire body of the Old Testament unveiled the coming Messiah, the Son of God, who every Jew looked for with great expectancy. Peter, by inspiration of the Holy Spirit, is saying that the experience that he and the other two disciples (James and John) witnessed—seeing Jesus transfigured, seeing Moses and Elijah, and hearing the audible voice of God—validated the written Word of God and made it more reliable.[29]

The word *sure* in the King James Version in First Peter 1, verse 19 from the Greek, is *bebaioō*, and means "to make firm, establish, confirm, make sure."[30] This same Greek word is used in Mark 16:19-20.

> *After saying these things, Jesus was lifted up into heaven and sat down at the place of honor at the right hand of God! And the apostles went out announcing the good news everywhere, as the Lord himself consistently worked with them,* **validating** *the message they preached with miracle-signs that accompanied them!* (TPT)

The word in the King James Version is "confirming" the Word with signs following.

The Greek word is *bebaios* and is describing how the signs following were establishing and making firm and sure the Word that was being preached. The reason this is so important is because God never intended for the written Word to exist independent of manifestations of power, and experiences and encounters with God, which actually validate the Word and make it more sure and real in our own understanding and lives.

This Word that we say we believe and stand on is not a dead, lifeless, powerless word! This Word, as written, preached, taught, and believed, is designed to be validated in our lives and in the lives of those with whom we share it with validating experiences of God's power, presence, and glory. Without the experience, the things we believe are what Peter described as *"cunningly devised fables"* (2 Pet. 1:16)

This leads me to give context to something that Jesus had to address where Thomas is concerned, so let's go to John 20:24-29.

> *Now Thomas, called the Twin, one of the twelve, was not with them when Jesus came. The other disciples therefore said to him, "We have seen the Lord." So he said to them, "Unless I see in His hands the print of the nails, and put my finger into the print of the nails, and put my hand into His side, I will not believe." And after eight days His disciples were again inside, and Thomas with them. Jesus came, the doors being shut, and stood in the midst, and said, "Peace to you!" Then He said to Thomas, "Reach your finger here, and look at My hands; and reach your hand here, and put it into My side. Do not be unbelieving, but believing."*
>
> *And Thomas answered and said to Him, "My Lord and my God!" Jesus said to him, "Thomas, because*

*you have seen Me, you have believed. Blessed are those
who have not seen and yet have believed."*

Thomas made a decision that he would not believe without
seeing and feeling something. That self-willed decision was
completely out of line with everything Thomas had already
experienced, heard, and learned for three years. For him to
make that kind of decision in the face of everything that Jesus
taught Thomas and all the other disciples, including the testimony and witness of the other disciples to Thomas of what
they knew from experience, was completely unacceptable.

I like *The Passion Translation* of verse 29, *"Jesus responded,
'Thomas, now that you've seen me, you believe. But there are those
who have never seen me with their eyes but have believed in me
with their hearts, and they will be blessed even more!'"*

Faith empowers us to believe in the reality of Jesus without
ever having seen or touched Him from a physical sense experience. The written Word, and especially the Word preached
or taught under the anointing of God, produces a faith that
is based upon a decision to believe it, independent of physical
sense information.

However, God never intended that our entire life be lived
with no validating experiences. Once we have believed and
received Jesus, the power of God and a living, real life of faith
should and will have a multitude of experiences that continually
validate what we have already accepted by pure, simple faith.

This leads me to take you to one of my favorite passages
of Scripture; it is actually the foundation and basis of the call

of God on my life going all the way back to 1977. Let's go to Hebrews 5:12-14.

> *For though by this time you ought to be teachers, you need someone to teach you again the first principles of the oracles of God; and you have come to need milk and not solid food. For everyone who partakes only of milk is unskilled in the word of righteousness, for he is a babe. But solid food belongs to those who are of full age, that is, those who by reason of use have their senses exercised to discern both good and evil.*

Take a look at verse 14 from *The Passion Translation:*

> *But solid food is for the mature, whose spiritual senses perceive heavenly matters. And they have been adequately trained by what they've experienced to emerge with understanding of the difference between what is truly excellent and what is evil and harmful.*

For the longest time I only considered this verse from the perspective of having my physical senses trained to discern between good and evil. And to a great degree that is exactly what has happened. My physical body, as a result of over forty years of living in obedience to the Lord, no longer desires things that are evil and destructive

But there is a deeper meaning in this passage that is important to grasp as well. Just as our physical body has the five senses, our spirit has senses as well. Our body was made for our spirit, not the other way around. Therefore, the physical senses correlate with our spirit's ability to sense things as well.

The primary function of our soul is to be the communicator and connector between our spirit and our body, interpreting physical information for spiritual use and spiritual information for physical use. Because we are usually focused on the natural or physical realm not the spiritual, we are not as developed in our spiritual senses as we should be.

The new birth put within us the ability to live our lives from the inside out, being led and instructed from within by the influence of the Holy Spirit dwelling in us. We can now, though habitual practice, develop our spiritual senses to a degree that we can know things that are not perceptible through the five physical senses. The primary ingredient that helps us to develop the spiritual senses is the Word of God.

John 6:63, *"It is the Spirit who gives life; the flesh profits nothing. The words that I speak to you are spirit, and they are life."* God's Word is spiritual, not natural. The apostle Paul expands on this theme in First Corinthians 2:6-16:

> *However, we speak wisdom among those who are mature, yet not the wisdom of this age, nor of the rulers of this age, who are coming to nothing. But we speak the wisdom of God in a mystery, the hidden wisdom which God ordained before the ages for our glory, which none of the rulers of this age knew; for had they known, they would not have crucified the Lord of glory. But as it is written: "Eye has not seen, nor ear heard, Nor have entered into the heart of man the things which God has prepared for those who love Him."*

But God has revealed them to us through His Spirit. For the Spirit searches all things, yes, the deep things of God. For what man knows the things of a man except the spirit of the man which is in him? Even so no one knows the things of God except the Spirit of God. Now we have received, not the spirit of the world, but the Spirit who is from God, that we might know the things that have been freely given to us by God.

These things we also speak, not in words which man's wisdom teaches but which the Holy Spirit teaches, comparing spiritual things with spiritual. But the natural man does not receive the things of the Spirit of God, for they are foolishness to him; nor can he know them, because they are spiritually discerned. But he who is spiritual judges all things, yet he himself is rightly judged by no one. For "who has known the mind of the Lord that he may instruct Him?" But we have the mind of Christ.

We can see that the emphasis that the apostle Paul is making in this passage is the spiritually mature believer is to live life from the inside out. We have a wisdom and a mind that is not limited to only what can be determined from an outside-in perspective. The Holy Spirit who dwells within us is able to reveal things to us that are not based upon a natural perspective, but are coming from the wisdom, perception, and discernment that is flowing from the head, Jesus.

Even Jesus Himself, when He was in His earthly walk, lived from the inside out. Notice how Isaiah described this in chapter 11, verses 1-3.

> *There shall come forth a Rod from the stem of Jesse, and a Branch shall grow out of his roots. The Spirit of the Lord shall rest upon Him, the Spirit of wisdom and understanding, The Spirit of counsel and might, the Spirit of knowledge and of the fear of the Lord. His delight is in the fear of the Lord, and He shall not judge by the sight of His eyes, nor decide by the hearing of His ears.*

Jesus lived with a complete dependence on the Holy Spirit and the ability of the Holy Spirit to reveal things to Him from the inside, independent of whatever information was coming from the five physical senses. He did not make decisions based upon what He saw with His eyes, nor did He make decisions based upon what He heard with His physical ears. He was influenced and led and made decisions based upon what the Holy Spirit revealed to Him.

This is why He stated in John 3:13 this powerful reality: *"No one has ascended to heaven but He who came down from heaven, that is, the Son of Man who is in heaven."* Jesus lived His life in two dimensions at the same time. He was highly aware of the spirit dimension from which He lived His life in the natural realm. He was living His life in constant fellowship with His Father and dealt with whatever was taking place around Him in the natural realm from that dimension. This is why He said He did only what the Father showed Him to do and said only what the Father told Him to say.

He lived from the spiritual dimension and approached every moment of every day from the awareness of the Father's influence. I like to say it this way, "He expressed His Father completely through His physical body." We can give expression to Jesus through our physical bodies, if we will live from the inside out, in total dependence on the Holy Spirit.

This type of living demands that we develop our spiritual senses and renew our minds to an inside-out orientation as the way to live life. This is completely opposite to the way we were trained before we were born again; sadly, for many of us, the influence of religion has done little or nothing to help us shift to that way of living since we were born again.

The reason developing our spiritual senses is so important, and why I am spending time to get you to think about this, is because in order for us to live as sons of God, working with Jesus as we are seated with Him in the heavenlies, we must become more highly aware of the spirit dimension. Notice what the apostle Paul wrote in Colossians 3:1-3.

> *If then you were raised with Christ, seek those things which are above, where Christ is, sitting at the right hand of God. Set your mind on things above, not on things on the earth. For you died, and your life is hidden with Christ in God.*

There are many wonderful translations of this passage. I want you to read these two versions and meditate upon the words that are communicated here. This first selection is from *The Passion Translation.*

> *Christ's resurrection is your resurrection too. This is why we are to yearn for all that is above, for that's where Christ sits enthroned at the place of all power, honor, and authority!* **Yes, feast on all the treasures of the heavenly realm and fill your thoughts with heavenly realities, and not with the distractions of the natural realm.** *Your crucifixion with Christ has severed the tie to this life, and now your true life is hidden away in God in Christ.*

My favorite rendering of this passage is by William Barclay.

> If then you have been raised to life with Christ, your heart must be set of the great realities of that heavenly sphere, where Christ is seated at the right hand of God. *Your constant concern must be with the heavenly realities, not with worldly trivialities. For you died to this world, and now you have entered with Christ into the secret life of God.*[31]

You may have heard the old saying, "You are so heavenly minded that you are no earthly good." We may even laugh at that sentiment, but the truth is just the opposite. We have been so earthly minded that we have been no heavenly good. Heaven needs the Body of Christ to become aware of our seating with Christ, and Jesus needs us to begin to function from that dimension of the spirit.

This is why we must be developing our spiritual senses. To work with Jesus and the Holy Spirit, we must be more tuned into the realm of the spirit and learn how to step into the different places of function that allow us to become an active participant in the Kingdom of God, working to expand Kingdom influence and the culture of Heaven in accordance with our constant prayer, *"Your kingdom come. Your will be done on earth as it is in heaven"* (Matt 6:10).

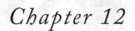

Chapter 12

SECURING THE DESTINIES OF NATIONS

I have endeavored to lay out an explanation in the previous chapters of why understanding the legal aspects of the devil's strategies is so important; because this is critical for us to see the bigger picture and purpose that God has called us to accomplish as we work with Him in the Courts of Heaven. We learn by securing our own future and destinies, but we should not be satisfied to accomplish that at the expense of letting the lion's share of Jesus's inheritance remain unsecured.

Because we are joint heirs with Christ, we have to understand that if we don't possess it, He can't control it or use it. Our possession of the earthly, material side of creation is not about securing a personal dimension of prosperity. It is to secure what Jesus died to bring under His control and influence that was lost through Adam's fall.

Let me illustrate this in this manner. Take notice of what the Lord reveals through Haggai 2:4-9:

"Yet now be strong, Zerubbabel," says the Lord; "and be strong, Joshua, son of Jehozadak, the high priest; and be strong, all you people of the land," says the Lord, "and work; for I am with you," says the Lord of hosts. "According to the word that I covenanted with you when you came out of Egypt, so My Spirit remains among you; do not fear!" For thus says the Lord of hosts: "Once more (it is a little while) I will shake heaven and earth, the sea and dry land; and **I will shake all nations, and they shall come to the Desire of All Nations, and I will fill this temple with glory," says the Lord of hosts. "The silver is Mine, and the gold is Mine," says the Lord of hosts. "The glory of this latter temple shall be greater than the former," says the Lord of hosts. "And in this place I will give peace," says the Lord of hosts.**

The setting of this word is when Haggai and Zechariah were helping the Jews to rebuild Jerusalem and the temple in Jerusalem. Notice what is found in Ezra 6:14:

So the elders of the Jews built, and they prospered through the prophesying of Haggai the prophet and Zechariah the son of Iddo. And they built and finished it, according to the commandment of the God of Israel,

*and according to the command of Cyrus, Darius, and
Artaxerxes king of Persia.*

Haggai and Zechariah were the two prophets who were
assisting the elders of Jerusalem as they were working to fulfill the mission of rebuilding Jerusalem and the temple after
returning from Babylonian captivity. While the physical work
was taking place, the prophets were keeping things on track
from the spiritual dimension.

The Lord, through Haggai, was addressing the fact that
the ultimate goal was the reclamation of the nations, and
right along with that the possession of the silver and the gold.
God's declaration should speak to the Body of Christ in giving
understanding that while God owns all the gold and all the
silver, actually very little of that gold and silver is under His
direct control or influence.

A quick side note here. The word *glory* actually speaks of
gold and silver as well as all material wealth. The definition
of the word *glory* is interesting in that its first use is of material wealth and riches (Gen. 31:1 KJV). Literally the word
means to be heavy with everything that is good, to be wealthy,
loaded down with abundance. God's manifested presence is
also connected to this word. God's glory is full and heavy with
everything that is good. When God's glory is manifested, it
will also produce a definite increase in material and financial
wealth. Just ask Solomon and Jesus!

I wanted to point out what Haggai said, and the time in
which he said it, because there is a major event that took place

that was behind the rebuilding efforts that is vitally pertinent to the subject of this book. Let's look at Zechariah 3:1-7.

> *Then he showed me Joshua the high priest standing before the Angel of the Lord, and Satan standing at his right hand to oppose him. And the Lord said to Satan, "The Lord rebuke you, Satan! The Lord who has chosen Jerusalem rebuke you! Is this not a brand plucked from the fire?"*
>
> *Now Joshua was clothed with filthy garments, and was standing before the Angel. Then He answered and spoke to those who stood before Him, saying, "Take away the filthy garments from him." And to him He said, "See, I have removed your iniquity from you, and I will clothe you with rich robes." And I said, "Let them put a clean turban on his head." So they put a clean turban on his head, and they put the clothes on him. And the Angel of the Lord stood by. Then the Angel of the Lord admonished Joshua, saying, "Thus says the Lord of hosts: 'If you will walk in My ways, and if you will keep My command, then you shall also judge My house, and likewise have charge of My courts; I will give you places to walk among these who stand here.'"*

It is interesting that the Hebrew word that is translated as satan in this passage should more accurately be translated as "adversary." The *Gesenius' Hebrew-Chaldee Lexicon to the Old Testament* describes this word as "adversary," and for the reference in Zechariah 3 the definition is applied as an adversary "in a court of justice."[32] This matches up perfectly with the way the word *adversary* is used in the New Testament, as we have already pointed out earlier.

The adversary is resisting Joshua, the high priest, from a legal position in the Court of Heaven. Joshua is wearing filthy garments, and this defilement is being used by the adversary as the basis of a case designed to hinder and stop the rebuilding of Jerusalem. Notice the declaration of the Lord to the adversary in verse 2: "*The Lord rebuke you, Satan! The Lord who has chosen Jerusalem rebuke you!*"

God had chosen Jerusalem, and the adversary was attempting to delay God's purposes for the city by using Joshua's defilement as the basis of his case against God's plans. This is vastly important for us to understand! Our earth walk must be continually perfected in holiness so that we are not providing our adversary avenues to use against the purposes of God in our lives, and even concerning the plans and purposes of cities, states, regions, and nations.

I want to reinforce that as new creation believers, we stand in the righteousness of God in our spirits; we are one spirit with the Lord. This union with Him is what allows us to deal with the things that defile us where our earth walk is concerned that can, and is used, by the adversary as a legal basis of resisting the purposes and plans of God. The revelation of dealing with sins, transgressions, and even bloodline iniquity in the Court of Heaven is not an exercise in sin consciousness; far from it! It is dealing with the legal issues that the adversary and accuser uses to thwart God's plans and purposes in the earth.

Notice what happened in this court case. The Lord commanded the angels standing by to remove the defiled garments off Joshua, Then the Lord said to Joshua, *"See, I have removed your iniquity from you, and I will clothe you with rich robes"* (v. 4). Zechariah, who was observing this, told the angels to put a clean turban on Joshua's head.

Removing Joshua's iniquity allowed the Angel of the Lord to declare unto Joshua this amazing statement, *"Thus says the Lord of hosts: 'If you will walk in My ways, and if you will keep My command, then you shall also judge My house, and likewise have charge of My courts; I will give you places to walk among these who stand here'"* (v. 7).

Joshua is being invited to be able to function in the court and do so in the role of a judge! He would have responsibility in the Courts of Heaven and would be working with the other spiritual beings that function in that courtroom with the Righteous Judge. This, once again, confirms that we, especially as born-again new creation beings, have the right and responsibility to function from our heavenly seating and conduct judicial business on behalf of the earth with respect to the plans and purposes of God as He designed it to fulfill Kingdom purpose!

The cleansing, purging, and purifying that we must engage in is dealing with our earth walk and our unredeemed physical body in order to position ourselves to be able to increase our effectiveness in God's Kingdom, which includes the Court of Heaven. This is essentially the putting off of the old man and putting on the new man that the apostle Paul repeatedly instructed believers to do in his letters to the church.

The ongoing cleansing of our lives from an earthly perspective is not automatic. We must take responsibility and continually pursue God's heart with a passion that energizes us to greater dimensions of purity and holiness, not from a legalistic, religious rule-keeping mind-set, but from a heart that desires to give the greatest expression of God as is possible while still living in these mortal physical bodies.

What is at stake? Literally nations hang in the balance! The Body of Christ is the "boots on the ground" for the Kingdom of God. It is our physical presence that gives God so much in the way of legal rights to accomplish His purposes in the earth. Jesus is the head of the Body and is the king of the Kingdom. He is also the high priest of a kingdom of priests, made up of new creation beings that are one spirit with Him.

It is our priestly function that is so important to the Courts of Heaven, and it is our kingly function that is critical to earth. Without the courts we would not have the means to secure the legal rights through our priesthood that Heaven needs to grant the judgments and decrees, that when executed into place, bring a manifestation of God's plans and purposes into the earth. Our oneness with Jesus Christ and His oneness with born-again men and women are what has to work together in Spirit-led and Spirit-directed words and actions to see the plans and purposes of God fulfilled. All of this has to do with operating according to that which is legal according to spiritual law.

When Jesus was in the earth, He was just one man, in one geographical location. He, essentially, was the only man who was in oneness with God and understood the laws of the spirit and the legal environment of the earth in which He was living. Also, He had to live in such a manner so as to avoid sinning the first time, and He had to recognize when the enemy was bringing temptation in an attempt to ensnare Him into breaking spiritual law, not just the Law of Moses. Thankfully, Jesus lived out His life here successfully.

Now, the Body of Christ is made up of many members worldwide. The Spirit of God dwells within every born-again believer and is attempting to lead, guide, and direct every member of the Body of Christ in such a way that we are all living in corporate yielded obedience to the head. There are many potential issues that can make this a difficult task; the first and foremost issue is that of living in a fallen world with a body of flesh that is corrupt, weak, and mortal. The desires of the flesh are constantly battling against the desires of our born-again spirits, and the only buffer that keeps the flesh in check is the degree to which each individual believer has renewed his or her mind to the Word of God. This establishes a basis of agreement from within to give the Holy Spirit a decided advantage in influencing our decisions to work with God instead of against God.

This is also why the cleansing, purging, and purifying process is so important. When we, as individual believers, are engaged in corralling the desires of the flesh, it provides an advantage in giving the Spirit of God more and more influence in the earth. At the same time, this reduces, on an ever-increasing basis, legal things with which the adversary can build cases to hinder God's plans and purposes in the earth.

Reducing the influence of iniquity, by eliminating self-willed words and actions in greater numbers of God's sons and daughters, provides a powerful governmental advantage in the earth through which the Kingdom of God can gain greater and greater influence over the nations and cultures of this world.

This is the ultimate purpose of accessing the Courts of Heaven; so that God, through the Ecclesia, is granted the legal right to do what needs to be done without the enemy resisting it in the courtroom. By taking matters to the Court of Heaven, we can effectively stop the enemy from hindering God's Kingdom purposes on the battlefield. This is what brings great favor to the Ecclesia, and puts the devil in a place of great disadvantage.

Each nation needs to have a group of believers who are developed in their faith and understand the finished work of redemption; they also know how to function in their heavenly priesthood to remove every legal case that is hindering God's plans and purposes in their own nation. They work with the Righteous Judge, Jesus Christ, who is also the head of the Church, and respond to His promptings. This is what the real Church is supposed to be accomplishing and the manner in which they are truly graced and called to function.

Churches that are learning to be Spirit-led in their prayers, ministry, and outreaches will begin to experience an exponential increase in their influence and effectiveness, because the Holy Spirit is conducting a God-ordained synchronicity where Heaven and earth are not operating independent of one another, but in harmony and agreement with one another.

Cities, counties, states, regions, nations, and entire cultural groups can only experience the power of God that results in real and substantive change for the better when the entire Body of Christ takes their place as the true sons of God and allows the Holy Spirit to lead and direct their earthly activities in accordance with God's plans and purposes. Any element of self-will defiles the earthly element of what God is dependent on using and must be cleansed and purified to keep the accuser and adversary from gaining a legal advantage which he can use to hinder and even stop God's Kingdom from expanding in the earth. This is why the revelation of the Courts of Heaven is so important in our day.

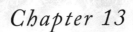

Chapter 13

STOP ACCEPTING DELAYS

I want to start this chapter off by making sure you understand my approach. The revelation of the New Testament is a progressive unveiling of truth. Isaiah 28:9-12 explains the way that God teaches us and reveals His Word to us.

> *"Whom will he teach knowledge? And whom will he make to understand the message? Those just weaned from milk? Those just drawn from the breasts? For precept must be upon precept, precept upon precept, line upon line, line upon line, here a little, there a little." For with stammering lips and another tongue He will speak to this people, to whom He said, "This is the rest with which you may cause the weary to rest," and, "This is the refreshing"; yet they would not hear.*

Notice God builds things in a gradual progression. Everything is connected, and in the light of the very first part of this passage, God's ability to bring greater light and understanding is dependent upon us growing up. Even the New Testament reveals that maturity demands that at some point we come off the milk and quit being babies.

The apostle Peter indicated that if you are a baby, then you need milk so that you will grow (1 Pet. 2:2), but the Apostle Paul explained in Hebrews 5:12-14 that once you start eating meat, you should no longer be acting like a baby and wanting milk.

> *For though by this time you ought to be teachers, you need someone to teach you again the first principles of the oracles of God; and you have come to need milk and not solid food. For everyone who partakes only of milk is unskilled in the word of righteousness, for he is a babe. But solid food belongs to those who are of full age, that is, those who by reason of use have their senses exercised to discern both good and evil.*

The apostle Paul also indicated in First Corinthians 3:1-3 that if you are acting like babies you are carnal and not spiritual, and essentially you are acting as if you aren't even born again.

> *And I, brethren, could not speak to you as to spiritual people but as to carnal, as to babes in Christ. I fed you with milk and not with solid food; for until now you were not able to receive it, and even now you are still not able; for you are still carnal. For where there*

are envy, strife, and divisions among you, are you not carnal and behaving like mere men?

I want you to notice that being a baby can provide the adversary plenty to work with where legal matters are concerned. Carnality is manifested in envy, strife, and divisions; being unskillful in the word of righteousness; and behavior that is not much different than that of "mere men," meaning those who are not born again and do not have the indwelling presence and power of the Holy Spirit.

Because the majority of the Body of Christ has been content to live as babies, entire doctrines have been fashioned to accommodate the inevitable delays that take place in people's lives; they attempt to believe God for things to happen, but they have not been taking care of the cases that have built up in the court from a lack of up-to-date repentance. God can do a lot of things for babies for a while. But there are things He cannot and will not be able to do once growth and maturity is expected and required.

One such teaching that has actually created a mind-set that gives the devil way too much opportunity to maneuver against us is an overemphasis of a statement from Ephesians 6:10-13.

Finally, my brethren, be strong in the Lord and in the power of His might. Put on the whole armor of God, that you may be able to stand against the wiles of the devil. For we do not wrestle against flesh and blood, but against principalities, against powers, against the rulers of the darkness of this age, against spiritual hosts of wickedness in the heavenly places. Therefore take up the whole armor of God, that you may be able to withstand in the evil day, and having done all, to stand.

I can tell you on the authority of God's Word that God never intended for us to have to "outlast" the devil while he attempts to "run out the clock" against us. The only reason the enemy has been able to get away with that is because we have functioned from a purely defensive mode of operation; in the light of what Jesus accomplished in the finished work and the nature and substance of our position in Heaven, we should not be allowing the clock to be used against us as a weapon.

I want to go back to Daniel 7:21-27, this time from the New American Standard Bible.

I kept looking, and that horn was waging war with the saints and overpowering them until the Ancient of Days came and judgment was passed in favor of the saints of the Highest One, and the time arrived when the saints took possession of the kingdom. "Thus he said: 'The fourth beast will be a fourth kingdom on the earth, which will be different from all the other kingdoms and will devour the whole earth and tread it down and crush it. As for the ten horns, out of this kingdom ten kings will arise; and another will arise after them, and he will be different from the previous ones and will subdue three kings. He will speak out against the Most High and wear down the saints

*of the Highest One, and he will intend to make alter-
ations in times and in law; and they will be given
into his hand for a time, times, and half a time. But
the court will sit for judgment, and his dominion will
be taken away, annihilated and destroyed forever.
Then the sovereignty, the dominion and the greatness
of all the kingdoms under the whole heaven will be
given to the people of the saints of the Highest One;
His kingdom will be an everlasting kingdom, and all
the dominions will serve and obey Him.'"*

I again acknowledge that Daniel is seeing into the future
here and seeing things play out during the time of the
Antichrist, but there is something he was also seeing that is
pertinent to our understanding today.

Notice that the tactic the enemy was using was to overpower the people of God and wear them out by using time
as a weapon, even to the point that he sought to make altera-
tions in time and in law. Notice also that each time the court
held a session, the enemy lost his advantage and ultimately was
completely destroyed as a result of a judgment begin given by
the court.

If this is talking about the Jewish people in the end times,
it is understandable that the devil would have an upper hand
because the people would not be born again and only functioning based upon the Abrahamic covenant. I can't say for
sure that is what this is addressing, but for the sake of consideration I bring that up.

I do know that for the Ecclesia, the new creation Body of Christ, we are at a distinct advantage due to the fact that we can operate in the Courts of Heaven through our heavenly priesthood and heavenly seating in that courtroom. We are one spirit with the Righteous Judge Himself! We can secure judgments against the adversary and shut down the accuser by accessing the blood of the Lamb and giving our testimony before the Court, securing our legal right to be free! Isaiah 54:17, "*No weapon that is formed against you will prosper; and every tongue that accuses you in judgment you will condemn. This is the heritage of the servants of the Lord, and their vindication is from Me,' declares the Lord*" (NASB).

This is not talking about someone talking bad about you at Walmart or at church. This is talking about the accusations and testimony that the adversary uses against you in the Court of Heaven. Your vindication is secured by using the word of righteousness skillfully in the court, knowing how to present your case, and executing the verdict already established by what Jesus did in His finished work of redemption. You have every right to condemn the legal maneuvers of the adversary when you know how to remove all the legal rights he is using against you.

Delay is never acceptable when dealing with the curse! We must refuse to accept the ability of the enemy to resist us with virtual impunity. We have to acknowledge that any steadfast resistance to our authority by the devil is an indicator that there might be something legal in nature that is giving him the right to stay and not flee. When this occurs, we need to shift from the battlefield and move to the Court of Heaven and remove the legal issues that are hindering our authority from being effective.

I don't think we realize that the enemy is constantly looking for ways to hinder and delay the purposes of God in the earth; he will go to great lengths to accomplish his mission. Look at First Thessalonians 2:17-18:

> *Beloved friends, we may have been torn away from you physically for a season, but never in our hearts. For we have had intense longings and have endeavored to come and see in your faces the reflection of this great love. We miss you badly, and I personally wanted to come to you, trying again and again, but our adversary, Satan, blocked our way* (TPT).

You can read in Acts 17 where the apostle Paul taught for three weeks in the synagogue in Thessalonica with some success. However, the religious Jews were moved with great envy against Paul and as a result, he and Silas ended up having to leave Thessalonica in the middle of the night out of concern for their safety. They went to Berea and then to Athens, where, it is agreed by many Bible scholars, that Paul wrote both letters to the believers at Thessalonica.

What is interesting to note is that this great apostle acknowledged that the adversary, satan, found a way to block him from being able to return to Thessalonica. Whether this was through human agency or through some other tactic, we see that the enemy was hindering the apostle Paul from returning to the area.

In recent times I have heard many believers make completely unsubstantiated and unbiblical statements that are completely out of touch with reality. One such statement is, "I have authority, and satan can't do anything to me!" I believe the apostle Paul would take exception to that statement. He wrote this in Second Corinthians 12:1-10:

> *It is doubtless not profitable for me to boast. I will come to visions and revelations of the Lord: I know a man in Christ who fourteen years ago—whether in the body I do not know, or whether out of the body I do not know, God knows—such a one was caught up to the third heaven. And I know such a man— whether in the body or out of the body I do not know, God knows—how he was caught up into Paradise and heard inexpressible words, which it is not lawful for a man to utter. Of such a one I will boast; yet of myself I will not boast, except in my infirmities. For though I might desire to boast, I will not be a fool; for I will speak the truth. But I refrain, lest anyone should think of me above what he sees me to be or hears from me. And lest I should be exalted above measure by the abundance of the revelations, a thorn in the flesh was given to me, a messenger of Satan to buffet me, lest I be exalted above measure. Concerning this thing I pleaded with the Lord three times that it might depart from me. And He said to me, "My grace is sufficient*

*for you, for My strength is made perfect in weakness."
Therefore most gladly I will rather boast in my infirmities, that the power of Christ may rest upon me.
Therefore I take pleasure in infirmities, in reproaches,
in needs, in persecutions, in distresses, for Christ's
sake. For when I am weak, then I am strong.*

This famous passage is where we find Paul referring to "the
thorn in the flesh" and that was attributed to coming from
the devil. God did not give Paul the thorn; satan was the one
who was the thorn. And we can find in Second Corinthians
11:18-28 the description of how this "thorn in the flesh" manifested in Paul's life and ministry.

*Seeing that many boast according to the flesh, I also
will boast. For you put up with fools gladly, since
you yourselves are wise! For you put up with it if one
brings you into bondage, if one devours you, if one
takes from you, if one exalts himself, if one strikes you
on the face. To our shame I say that we were too weak
for that! But in whatever anyone is bold—I speak
foolishly—I am bold also. Are they Hebrews? So am
I. Are they Israelites? So am I. Are they the seed of
Abraham? So am I. Are they ministers of Christ?—I
speak as a fool—I am more: in labors more abundant,
in stripes above measure, in prisons more frequently,
in deaths often. From the Jews five times I received
forty stripes minus one. Three times I was beaten with
rods; once I was stoned; three times I was shipwrecked;
a night and a day I have been in the deep; in journeys*

often, in perils of waters, in perils of robbers, in perils of my own countrymen, in perils of the Gentiles, in perils in the city, in perils in the wilderness, in perils in the sea, in perils among false brethren; in weariness and toil, in sleeplessness often, in hunger and thirst, in fastings often, in cold and nakedness—besides the other things, what comes upon me daily: my deep concern for all the churches.

These are all things that were manifestations of the "thorn in the flesh." These are all the things that satan was doing to try and stop the apostle Paul from accomplishing his mission and fulfilling his purposes.

God's response to Paul's request to have this "thorn" removed is interesting, *"Concerning this thing I pleaded with the Lord three times that it might depart from me. And He said to me, 'My grace is sufficient for you, for My strength is made perfect in weakness'"* (vv. 8-9).

Apparently, God was communicating that He had given Paul grace to deal with the thorn himself. That grace came to bring a strength to bear that only worked as Paul acknowledged his total dependency on that grace. If you look at *Thayer's Greek-English Lexicon* you will see that the word *perfect* in Second Corinthians 12:9 is rendered this way, "my power shows itself most efficacious in them that are weak."[33]

Why would it be this way? Because we cannot "resist" the devil in our own strength or power; nor can we resist the devil out of our own initiative. It is when we are completely yielded to the head, Jesus Christ, that we are at our strongest where satan is concerned. Again, self-willed resistance is powerless against the one who gave birth to self-will!

We have a very real and dangerous enemy. He functions continually in the unseen realm of the spirit, and the Bible describes him as cunning, crafty, subtle, and the sum of wisdom. He didn't lose all that wisdom when he lost his first estate, although his wisdom is now corrupted by pride and iniquity. He has been the one responsible for over six thousand years for all the death, destruction, and misery inflicted upon mankind. He is not to be made fun of in some kind of derisive, slanderous way. This leads to believers being less than sober and vigilant to be ever watchful and aware of his strategies and schemes. As the Lord spoke to me just recently, "Bill, slander of the devil is not equal to resistance of the devil!"

No, we are to resist the devil by being steadfast in the faith. We do this by being led by the Holy Spirit in everything we do and say. This will lead us to resisting on many occasions through spiritual warfare, and on other occasions we will be led to the Courts of Heaven. Both manners of activity and operations are how we exercise our authority and resist the devil. But the key to using the proper strategy is listening to the Holy Spirit and learning to recognize what strategy the enemy is employing against you at the time.

No army can win a war without proper intelligence of the enemy's activities; having right strategy employed to engage the enemy, maximizes their strengths and exploits the enemy's weaknesses. No army can survive in the field without constant contact with headquarters and following orders as given by those who see the bigger picture of what is going on at the moment.

This is a picture of what the Body of Christ is to function like in the earth. Jesus is the commander in chief and the Holy Spirit is the communicator and link between us and head-quarters. The angels, in many ways, are the intelligence corps and are involved in supply and support. The command structure of the Body of Christ is designed to keep things flowing and functioning in agreement with the overall plans and purposes of the Kingdom of God. The Body is also called to help assist Jesus in the training and equipping of every member of the army of the Lord while in the earth. Independent actions of any member can introduce confusion at best, and at worst, can allow the enemy to gain advantage in ways that can lead to frustration and defeat.

This is why the Courts of Heaven is such an important revelation as we enter into these last days. This is not a form or style of prayer; it is a very realm aspect of the Kingdom of God, a dimension of Heaven that every born-again believer is able to access and function from to bring the earthly agreement and participation needed to legally execute the plans and purposes of God as He designed them to be carried out.

Chapter 14

TAKE THE FIRST STEP

I want to encourage you to take the first step and use your faith to enter into the Courts of Heaven; take advantage of all that the Court can do to bring the plans and purposes of God into manifestation in ways and on levels unlike anything you have experienced before. Don't fall prey to the tendency to want to "know everything" about this before you start taking advantage of working with Jesus as the Righteous Judge.

I want to share a few thoughts that will help you going into the Court and knowing what to expect. There is nothing to fear in that courtroom. If you look at the description throughout the Old and New Testaments, the Court of Heaven is set up for us to function there and work with Jesus. That is nothing to fear; there is something to look forward to with great expectancy!

You are not stepping into the Court to be judged. You are going there to remove any legal things that the adversary is using against you, and that is a good thing. Jesus, as the Righteous Judge, wants and needs you to do this. The only one who would not want you to go to court is the devil. If the truth is known, the devil is not at all happy that the revelation of the Courts of Heaven has been released to the Body of Christ.

The Holy Spirit is your greatest help when you step into the Court. He is called our Advocate for a reason. The Greek word is *parakletos*, and means "one who pleads another's cause before a judge, a pleader, counsel for defense, legal assistant, an advocate."[34] Another word used for this function of the Holy Spirit is *comforter*, as one who is called to one's side to offer aid or assistance. There are many other definitions of this word, but the primary use of *parakletos* was always in the context of one who helped a defendant in a court of justice.

The Holy Spirit knows His way around that courtroom! He will lead you to say the right things, and He will help you to know and perceive what needs to be dealt with so that you come out of every case having accomplished what needed to be accomplished to further the purposes of God in your life. You will find that the more you go to court, the more intense and intimate your relationship with the Holy Spirit will become; that is a good thing!

There is absolutely no guilt or condemnation in that courtroom. This is one of the most outstanding things I noticed as I began to function in the Court of Heaven. Jesus will never condemn you! The Holy Spirit will never make you feel guilty!

Even on those occasions when I work with a seer gift to deal with things on a different level, the most outstanding characteristic of learning what needed to be dealt with in terms of sin, transgression, or iniquity is that, there was never a sense of guilt or condemnation. There was only a great desire to remove the legal issues so that the will of God could be accomplished or realized.

This is not an exercise in sin consciousness. You are not on a witch hunt; you are discovering the things that the enemy has been using legally to hinder, delay, or deny your rights secured by Jesus through the finished work of redemption or what is written in your heavenly book of destiny. Every time I complete a time in the Court, there is a sense that I am now able to function at a higher level of faith and effectiveness, never with a greater awareness of consciousness of sin.

Just remember that it is because you are a new creation in Christ and have been already made the very righteousness of God through your union with Christ that you are able to step into the Court of Heaven and access all that is available to you there. You are welcome there.

Also, don't be concerned that you may make a mistake or say or do something wrong while you are in court. The Holy Spirit will assist you; and Jesus, as the Righteous Judge, is gracious, kind, and patient. You will learn much each time you go to court, and you don't have to be a legal expert on how a courtroom works to be successful.

Pay attention to the what your spirit and senses are picking up on while you are in Court. You don't have to have a seer to see what is going on, and your spiritual hearing will be sharpened the more you go to court.

On this point, I have to say that when I first started going to court, those first several times I stepped out by faith, I didn't see anything, and I heard very little. That began to change after a few months; now, I see and hear very clearly almost every time I go to court. I have seen Jesus, angels, and even different individuals from the heavenly cloud of witnesses. There have been a few occasions when I have seen the adversary and representatives of the realm of darkness who were required to show up for the cases I was handling. This was never a contrived figment of my imagination, but a very real function of the ability to see and know things that are taking place in the realm of the spirit that every born-again believer has the ability and capacity to develop.

One thing I can say with all confidence and assurance is that every time I have gone to court, things have changed. There have been instances when the changes were not evident right away in the natural realm, but things did change regardless. Sometimes it is like peeling an onion, one layer at a time, with nothing much happening to indicate progress. And then, all of a sudden, you will do some work in the Court on an issue you have been working through for several days, and all kinds of things start happening in the natural realm.

Several times I have witnessed change within twenty-four hours. On one occasion I was assisting a minister friend within a series of court visits over a period of several days. The Holy Spirit was revealing things to me, and I would tell my friend what to do when he stepped into the Court of Heaven to stop what the devil had planned to do. This had been one of those situations when we had been peeling a legal onion that had actually developed over a period of years. The devil thought he had built an ironclad case to steal this man's ministry and destroy a major player in the Kingdom of God. One afternoon the Holy Spirit revealed a major legal issue that needed to be removed, and within forty-five minutes of my friend taking care of that one issue, a person who was a key player in the situation came into his office and repented of wrong attitudes and behavior!

My point is this, don't be moved if things don't change in a short time frame, especially if there are a lot of people involved. God will not overpower people's will. But know and understand that when you remove the legal things that the adversary may be using to hinder the purposes of God, there will come a point, sooner and not later, that things will start shifting in the natural realm.

Keep your own repentance list as short as possible. Don't be slow to forgive people. Be quick to repent and confess your sins according to First John 1:9. You know when you have sinned and transgressed; don't act like you don't know what I'm talking about! We all have times that our flesh gets the best of us, and we do or say things that we know we shouldn't. Repent!

Where iniquity in the bloodline is concerned, you can gain a pretty good understanding about the legal issues the adversary is using to hinder and delay, especially where healing or finances is concerned. You know the family traits that exist that are not in alignment or agreement with the Kingdom of God and the instruction of the New Testament. By faith, offer repentance for those things in the court; ask that the blood of Jesus be allowed to speak on your family's behalf and have all the legal issues connected to those things removed.

Ask the Holy Spirit to reveal to you the things the adversary is using to hinder, delay, or deny what the Word of God clearly states that you or your born-again family members have a right to receive or walk in. Whatever the Holy Spirit reveals to you, repent before the Righteous Judge for those things and ask that on the basis of Colossians 2:14 that every legal thing the adversary is using to hang things up be completely removed and remitted by the blood of the Lamb.

You can ask for your book of destiny to be opened and for judgments and decrees be granted based upon what is in your book. This is based upon Psalm 139:14-16.

> *I thank you, God, for making me so mysteriously complex! Everything you do is marvelously breathtaking. It simply amazes me to think about it!*
>
> *How thoroughly you know me, Lord! You even formed every bone in my body when you created me in the secret place, carefully, skillfully shaping me from nothing to something. You saw who you created me to be before I became me! Before I'd ever seen the light of day, the number of days you planned for me were already recorded in your book* (TPT).

Every person ever born has a book in Heaven that is written by God concerning His plans and purposes for their lives. In fact, everything that has Kingdom purposes attached to it has a book in Heaven.[35]

We can find the essence of what is in your own book by seeing how God's plans are described in Ephesians 2:10.

> *For we are God's [own] handiwork (His workmanship), recreated in Christ Jesus, [born anew] that we may do those good works which God predestined (planned beforehand) for us [taking paths which He prepared ahead of time], that we should walk in them [living the good life which He prearranged and made ready for us to live]* (AMPC).

This is a description of the marvelous and wonderful plan and purposes that God created you to fulfill; all of it is written in your own personal book of destiny. That book and what it describes is what the adversary is wanting to keep from happening.

All of the legal issues that he brings in the form of lawsuits and accusations are things that he wants to use to keep you from realizing and experiencing the amazing life that God originally purposed for you to live out in this earth. The reason the devil fights this so hard is because your successful realization of this plan hastens the devil's unavoidable day of judgment. The longer he can put off the Body of Christ, in general, and you and me specifically, from living out of the fullness of our book, the longer he can delay that day.

It is for this reason that Daniel saw that when the court was in session, the books were open. The court deals with the legal issues related to what is in the books. Verdicts, judgments, and decrees are all part of what the court exists to legally put into force. The Body of Christ is to take those things, once secured, and execute them into place in the earth.

As I have already said, Jesus did what He did in His suffering, death, resurrection, and ascension to secure the greatest verdict ever rendered by the heavenly supreme court. That verdict secured the right to enjoy the life that God designed and predetermined for every person who would ever be born. The enemy of mankind, and of God, works continually—both legally and illegally—to keep that from happening.

The Body of Christ has been brought into a living union with Jesus Christ so that we can function in that heavenly court when necessary. And as duly deputized officers of the Court, we can execute the verdicts and judgments secured in that court into place in this earth.

No doubt, there is a need to deal with the enemy on the battlefield, mostly when he is attempting to do something illegally. But in this day, Heaven needs God's sons and daughters to use the Courts of Heaven to fight for our joint inheritance with Jesus and remove the legal issues that the adversary has been using to keep that inheritance from coming under Jesus's control.

Here is something to keep in mind. Jesus has already inherited, through His work of redemption, all things. We, as His Body in the earth, must take possession of His inheritance.

The Courts of Heaven allow us, as His earthly representatives and spiritual body, to deal with all the legal issues that the adversary uses to keep things from coming into our possession and under Jesus's control. Jesus cannot accomplish that independent of us, but through us by His Holy Spirit. That is why the Courts of Heaven are so important, and why He needs us to work in both realms to secure what He died to save, which is the entirety of creation and of the human family.

Chapter 15

THREE FORMS OF
SIN AND THEIR
LEGAL CLAIM

By Robert Henderson

When we consider the whole idea of iniquity this can be a mysterious thing. The Bible even refers to the *mystery of iniquity*. Second Thessalonians 2:7 says this mystery is working right now.

> *For the mystery of lawlessness is already at work; only He who now restrains will do so until He is taken out of the way.*

It is my persuasion that the devil uses iniquity as a legal right to resist the purposes of God in our lives. In fact, this is why so many of God's people have been unable to come into the breakthrough they know is intended for them. They feel like there is a bungee cord tied to their back. As they try to move forward it is with great effort, only to be pulled back into a place they are trying to get free from. This has created a great frustration and at times even a resolve to just give up and maintain. However, if we can discern the *mystery* surrounding iniquity and through the Holy Spirit's wisdom and empowerment undo it, we can move fully into what the Lord has for us.

Iniquity is a form of sin. In fact, David listed iniquity as one of the three ideas concerning sin in Psalm 32:1-2.

> *Blessed is he whose transgression is forgiven,*
> *Whose sin is covered.*
> *Blessed is the man to whom the Lord does not impute*
> *iniquity,*
> *And in whose spirit there is no deceit.*

Sin in the Hebrew is word *chataah*. It means to "offend." So, our *sin* is when we offend God. If you go deep enough into the meaning of this word, you will find it means "to miss." In other word, we *miss* the target of holiness and righteousness. When we do, this *offends* God. Sin is an attack on the very nature of God. This is why we are told to not grieve the Holy Spirit we have been sealed with. Ephesians 4:29-32 tells us there is certain conduct that can cause the Spirit of God to be grieved as a result of our offense.

Let no corrupt word proceed out of your mouth, but what is good for necessary edification, that it may impart grace to the hearers. And do not grieve the Holy Spirit of God, by whom you were sealed for the day of redemption. Let all bitterness, wrath, anger, clamor, and evil speaking be put away from you, with all malice. And be kind to one another, tenderhearted, forgiving one another, even as God in Christ forgave you.

It seems like our words and attitudes toward others can cause this grief of the Holy Spirit. The word *grieve* is the Greek word *lupeo*. It means "to distress or to make sad." It is possible for the Spirit of God, as God Himself to be saddened by our activity and sin. We can offend Him. If you have the Holy Spirit living in you, you will feel His sadness and grieve at the words that come from your mouth. He will cause a guard to be set on your mouth that will restrain words that would otherwise be spoken. We must repent where we might have violated this restraint. "May the words of my mouth and the meditations of my heart, be acceptable to You O Lord (see Psalm 19:14). *Sin* is, at its root, against the holiness of God. This is important to know.

David also spoke of transgression as being a form of trespassing against the Lord. This is the Hebrew word *pesha*. It means "a revolt or to break away from just authority," *rebellion*. Whereas *sin* is about morality, *transgression* is about rebellion. There is a difference between moral sins and the sins of rebellion. One is a sin against God's holiness, while the other, transgression, is a sin against the authority of God. One seems to carry a greater punishment than the other. It appears that *transgression*, which is about *breaking away from just authority*, has greater consequences. This could be because it is the *original sin*. For example, sin against the authority of God, transgression, was what satan, the devil, was guilty of. Isaiah 14:12-15 shows that lucifer's desire to exalt himself was what got him kicked out of heaven.

> *How you are fallen from heaven,*
> *O Lucifer, son of the morning!*
> *How you are cut down to the ground,*
> *You who weakened the nations!*
> *For you have said in your heart:*
> *"I will ascend into heaven,*
> *I will exalt my throne above the stars of God;*
> *I will also sit on the mount of the congregation*
> *On the farthest sides of the north;*
> *I will ascend above the heights of the clouds,*
> *I will be like the Most High."*
> *Yet you shall be brought down to Sheol,*
> *To the lowest depths of the Pit.*

Satan's intent, or lucifer as he was known in heaven, was to ascend and exalt his throne and *be like* the Most High. This was rebellion against the authority of God. When we rebel against authority, this is a serious sin. We are even warned about it in the writings of Paul to Timothy in First Timothy

3:6 when Paul is instructing about who should be a leader in the church and who should not.

> *...not a novice, lest being puffed up with pride he fall into the same condemnation as the devil.*

Paul warns that a novice or one that is a young believer, shouldn't be placed in this position of authority or what happened to satan could happen to them. They could come into the same judgment that lucifer fell under because of pride developing in their heart. They could actually revolt and/or stir up a revolt against the God-ordained and set authority in the church. This is what satan did that caused him to be removed from his place in heaven. He didn't just rebel himself, he caused a great rebellion among a third of the angels of heaven. (See Revelation 12:4.) This is what Paul is alluding to concerning someone falling into the condemnation of the devil. Giving positions of authority and influence should always we done with much gravity and examination. Otherwise problems can arise later because of something being done prematurely.

Sins against the holiness of God are serious. Trespasses against the authority of God would appear to be perhaps even more so. First Corinthians 10:6-10 list some of the sins the people were guilty of in the wilderness that caused serious consequences. As the people of God journeyed to the promise land, they sinned some great sins.

> *Now these things became our examples, to the intent that we should not lust after evil things as they also lusted. And do not become idolaters as were some of*

them. As it is written, "The people sat down to eat and drink, and rose up to play." Nor let us commit sexual immorality, as some of them did, and in one day twenty-three thousand fell; nor let us tempt Christ, as some of them also tempted, and were destroyed by serpents; nor complain, as some of them also complained, and were destroyed by the destroyer.

From this list of five things that judgment came on, it would appear two were sins against God's holiness while three were sins against His authority. *Lusting and sexual immorality* would definitely be in the "sin against the holiness of God" category. However, *idolatry, tempting Christ and complaining* would be in the "sin against the authority of the Lord" category. There were results from both. One of the greatest judgments was against Korah and his company that rebelled against Moses and Aaron as God's delegated authority. Numbers 16:31-34 chronicles the judgment that came on Korah, his house and all those who aligned with him.

Now it came to pass, as he finished speaking all these words, that the ground split apart under them, and the earth opened its mouth and swallowed them up, with their households and all the men with Korah, with all their goods. So they and all those with them went down alive into the pit; the earth closed over them, and they perished from among the assembly. Then all Israel who were around them fled at their cry, for they said, "Lest the earth swallow us up also!"

God visibly judged this rebellion against His authority. They didn't realize that when they rebelled against Moses and Aaron, they were in actuality rebelling against God. We must be very careful or we can be guilty of the same. Remember that *transgression* is the *rebellion against just authority*. In other words, it is authority that God has set and we are to honor even as we would honor God Himself. This is why Romans 13:1-2 exhorts us to walk humbly and wisely before all authority:

> *Let every soul be subject to the governing authorities. For there is no authority except from God, and the authorities that exist are appointed by God. Therefore, whoever resists the authority resists the ordinance of God, and those who resist will bring judgment on themselves.*

This scripture says that *all authority* is from God. This doesn't mean that *all authority* is representing who God is. It does mean, however, that they are in authority because the position they occupy is from God. When we honor authority, we are in fact honoring God. If, however, we rebel against authority, we are rebelling against God. When the earth opened up and swallowed Korah and his company the people began to cry out in fear that they too would be swallowed. This was because they realized they were guilty of the same sin as Korah. They too had murmured and complained. They too had spoken against Moses and Aaron. They too had felt they had a right to express their opinion about matters. The problem was this was all against God's set authority. This can be very serious with the Lord. Remember that when Aaron and Miriam, who were Moses' natural brother and sister, spoke against Moses in Numbers 12:1-2 God called them into account:

> *Then Miriam and Aaron spoke against Moses because of the Ethiopian woman whom he had married; for he had married an Ethiopian woman. So they said, "Has the Lord indeed spoken only through Moses? Has He not spoken through us also?" And the Lord heard it.*

Those words, *"And the Lord heard it,"* should put a shudder in us. Wow. Miriam and Aaron just thought they were griping about their older brother. They were saying to each other, *"We're just as good as Moses. Besides, we don't like his new wife. She's not even Jewish. Moses isn't supposed to marry her. She's outside the Jewish people."* This actually was correct. The problem was, Moses' activity, whether sin or not, wasn't as important to God as the murmuring against God's authority was. This was clearly the greater sin! God calls Aaron, Miriam, and Moses to come out for little chat. He's going to deal with this family squabble. I'm sure Miriam and Aaron think Moses is about to get it. He's wrong. His wife is the wrong race, color and from the wrong traditions and cultures. They didn't understand the way God saw things. Numbers 12:6-9 shows us what the Lord said:

> *Then He said,*
> *"Hear now My words:*
> *If there is a prophet among you,*

I, the Lord, make Myself known to him in a vision;
I speak to him in a dream.
Not so with My servant Moses;
He is faithful in all My house.
I speak with him face to face,
Even plainly, and not in dark sayings;
And he sees the form of the Lord.
Why then were you not afraid
To speak against My servant Moses?"
So the anger of the Lord was aroused against them,
and He departed.

God doesn't correct Moses, even though He might have in secret. We do know however that He does correct Miriam and Aaron severely. Miriam is struck and made leprous on the spot. Aaron cries to Moses to please beseech the Lord to heal their sister. Moses in his humility does just this. God heals her but tells Moses that she needs to bear a reproach for what she has done. Numbers 12:13-15 show that she had to stay outside the camp for seven days.

So Moses cried out to the Lord, saying, "Please heal
her, O God, I pray!"
Then the Lord said to Moses, "If her father had but
spit in her face, would she not be shamed seven days?
Let her be shut out of the camp seven days, and after-
ward she may be received again." So Miriam was

shut out of the camp seven days, and the people did not journey till Miriam was brought in again.

The whole nation was stopped from journeying as a result of this. The idea is that griping and complaining against God's delegated authority that represents Him can stop us from moving forward. The reproach we bear from such issues can hinder the movement of an entire people. This was the consequence of not a sin against God's holiness, but rather against His authority. It could be argued that Moses marrying the Ethiopian woman was a sin against God's holiness. This brought no response from God that we can see. However the sin against the authority of God did. This is *transgression*. (By the way, as far as I'm concerned God has no problem with interracial marriages. This was only in regards to God's standard for that time in regards to marriage within the Jewish race.)

The other kind of sin David mentioned was iniquity. In the Hebrew this is the word *avon*. It means a "perversity or to be crooked." Iniquity is the sin that is in the bloodline! It is the history of sin that causes things to be twisted. This is why Nehemiah and others repented not only for their personal sin but also the iniquity of the fathers. Nehemiah 9:34 shows Nehemiah acknowledging the sin within the history of Israel that had allowed them to be in their current devastating condition.

Neither our kings nor our princes,
Our priests nor our fathers,
Have kept Your law,

Nor heeded Your commandments and Your testimonies,
With which You testified against them.

The commandments of God were testifying against them because they had not kept them. When we obey the word of the Lord, it testifies for us. When we break His word, it testifies against us. This is why the scripture says in Deuteronomy 30:19 that heaven and earth is called as a witness against us.

I call heaven and earth as witnesses today against you, that I have set before you life and death, blessing and cursing; therefore choose life, that both you and your descendants may live.

There were witnesses speaking that the right information was understood. The commandments given would either speak for them or against them, depending on obedience or disobedience. When Nehemiah prayed, he acknowledged that kings, priest, princes and forefathers had not kept the law. The result was a testimony against them. This is the history of sin or *iniquity* speaking against us. The result can be a case in the spirit world in the Court of Heaven that will not allow breakthrough to come. We must deal with this as well as sin and transgression. Any or all of these can work against us to hold us from our divine destiny, purpose and future.

Iniquity means something is crooked as we said. Iniquity in the bloodline will cause a perverting of desires and direction if not dealt with. There are two main forces that I can see in scripture that create desire and direction. One is from God, the other is used by the devil to pervert and twist. The one from God is in the books of destiny in Heaven. We all have these. Psalm 139:16 shows that our substance and days were written down before time began.

> *Your eyes saw my substance, being yet unformed.*
> *And in Your book they all were written,*
> *The days fashioned for me,*
> *When as yet there were none of them.*

This means that before I ever existed in the earth, there was a book in Heaven about me. The desires I have for my life, destiny and future should come out of this book. They are prophetic in nature. This is one of the main ways I know what is in my book. I can pay attention to my desire and discern this. Philippians 2:13 tells me that God fashions my desires in connection to His divine will and purpose.

> *...for it is God who works in you both to will and to*
> *do for His good pleasure.*

This wasn't decided by God today. This was determined ages ago in eternity. Then it was written in a book. We know this is true because of Ephesians 2:10 and Second Timothy 1:9.

> *For we are His workmanship, created in Christ Jesus*
> *for good works, which God prepared beforehand that*
> *we should walk in them.*
> *...who has saved us and called us with a holy calling,*
> *not according to our works, but according to His own*
> *purpose and grace which was given to us in Christ*
> *Jesus before time began.*

These verses show that what I was put in the earth to accomplish was *prepared beforehand*. This means what Psalm 139:16 states about the books. My days unfashioned and substance unformed were written down and recorded. Also *purpose and grace* were appointed to me *before time began*. So clearly the desires that God forms in me are connected to the purpose He wrote for me in His book. However the devil would want to pervert that sense of purpose and destiny. He does this through iniquity. He uses the iniquity in the bloodline not just to build cases against me but also to seek to thwart me from my divine destiny. He twists and makes crooked desires and longings that will lead me away from my divine order. This is why our own lust can lead us away from God's will. First Peter 4:1-2 shows this can and does happen:

> *Therefore, since Christ suffered for us in the flesh, arm yourselves also with the same mind, for he who has suffered in the flesh has ceased from sin, that he no longer should live the rest of his time in the flesh for the lusts of men, but for the will of God.*

There is a battle raging. Will I live the rest of my time for the lust of men or for the will of God? The deciding factor is whether I am letting what is in my book create a prophetic sense of destiny or the iniquity in the bloodline twist and contort my desires. When we deal with iniquity in the bloodline, this thing designed to make desires crooked will lose it powers. The thing we were made for, will take control over my life. Of course, we can see the significance of iniquity in the bloodline when we look at repeating generational patterns. For instance,

241

alcoholism and/or drug addiction are huge issues. It seems that almost always when this is a problem you find it to be generational in nature. If fathers, mothers and other people in our generations struggled with these issues, this can create the same scenario in a present generation. The devil uses the propensity toward these things through iniquity in the bloodline to tempt in this given arena. We see what the Bible calls the *desolation of many generations* set in motion (Isaiah 61:4). These issues tend to afflict and grow in severity from generation to generation. Why is this true. The devil uses the legal right of what was allowed in previous generations to tempt in a present generation. Therefore, instead of the desires coming from the books in Heaven concerning us, they become twisted by the desires driven through iniquity. We see this with mental illness, depression, anger, sexual perversion and a host of other things. That which has never been learned behavior finds its way into our lives and can began to dominate us. This is iniquity at work. The devil is taking advantage of the iniquity to twist and contort godly desires from the books of Heaven.

As we learn how to deal with these three forms of sin, we can quieten every legal case against us. Sin, or the offending of God's holiness. Transgression, or the rebellion and sin against the authority of God. Iniquity, the history of sin that perverts and twist desires away from God's plan for our lives. All of these can lose their power. Their legal right to operate can be revoked. God is faithful to His Word and will honor the work of His Son in our behalf. All we need to be free, successful and flourishing has been provided for us. God is good and we will see His goodness in the land of the living!

NOTES

CHAPTER 1: THE FINISHED WORK OF REDEMPTION

1. Brian Simmons, *Romans: Grace and Glory*, *The Passion Translation* (Racine, WI: BroadStreet Publishing Group, LLC, 2015), 28.

2. Clarence Jordan, *Clarence Jordan's Cotton Patch Gospel: Hebrews and the General Epistles* (Macon, GA: Smyth & Helwys Publishing, Inc., 2004), 41.

CHAPTER 2: THE ROOTS OF INIQUITY

3. A. S. Worrell, *The Worrell New Testament: A. S. Worrell's Translation With Study Notes* (Springfield, MO: Gospel Publishing House, 1904).

4. Simmons, *Romans: Grace and Glory*, 28.

5. Worrell, *The Worrell New Testament*.

CHAPTER 3: THE LEGALITY OF BLOOD

6. J. W. C. Wand, *The New Testament Letters, Prefaced and Paraphrased* (London: Oxford University Press, 1946), 106.

7. Robert Henderson, *Operating in the Courts of Heaven* (Waco, TX: Robert Henderson Ministries, 2014), 55.

8. Henderson, *Operating in the Courts of Heaven*,18-19.

9. Blue Letter Bible, s.v. *"antidikos,"* accessed September 2, 2019, https://www.blueletterbible.org/lang/lexicon/lexicon.cfm?Strongs=G476&t=KJV.

Chapter 5: What Is Bloodline Iniquity?

10. William Barclay, *The New Testament, A New Translation, Vol. 2, the Letters and the Revelation* (London: Collins, 1969), 207.

11. Caroline Leaf, *Switch on Your Brain* (Grand Rapids, MI: Baker Books, 2013).

Chapter 6: Becoming a Vessel of Honor

12 Noah Webster, *A Dictionary of the English Language* (New York: Harper & Brothers, 1845), s.v. "transmutation."

13. Bible Study Tools, s.v. *"katharizo,"* accessed September 2, 2019, https://www.biblestudytools.com/lexicons/greek/kjv/katharizo .html.

Chapter 7: The Mystery of Iniquity

14. James Strong, *Strong's Exhaustive Concordance Updated and Expanded Edition* (Peabody, MA: Hendrickson Publishers, 2007), s.v. "anomia."

15. Bible Hub, s.v. *"helkó,"* accessed September 3, 2019, https://biblehub.com/greek/1670.htm.

16. Bible Hub, s.v. *"haireó,"* accessed September 3, 2019, https://biblehub.com/greek/138.htm.

17. Blue Letter Bible, s.v. *"exaitéomai,"* accessed September 3, 2019, https://www.blueletterbible.org/lang/lexicon/lexicon.cfm?Strongs=G1809&t=KJV.

18. Blue Letter Bible, s.v. *"siniázō,"* accessed September 3, 2019, https://www.blueletterbible.org/lang/lexicon/lexicon .cfm?strongs=G4617.

CHAPTER 9: MY STORY OF FREEDOM FROM INIQUITY

19. Brian Simmons, *John: Eternal Love*, *The Passion Translation* (Racine, WI: BroadStreet Publishing Group, LLC, 2014), 47.

20. John Ayto, *Dictionary of Word Origins* (London: A & C Black Publisher Ltd., 2005), s.v. "religion," 419.

21. Ayto, *Dictionary of Word Origins*, 419.

CHAPTER 10: PROBATING THE NEW TESTAMENT INHERITANCE

22. *Webster's Dictionary 1828*, s.v. "destroy," accessed March 14, 2019, http://webstersdictionary1828.com/Dictionary/destroy.

23. W. E. Vine, Merrill F. Unger, and William White Jr., *Vine's Expository Dictionary of New Testament Words* (Old Tappan, NJ: Fleming H. Revell Co., 1996), s.v. "abolish," 13.

24. Vine, Unger, and White, *Vine's Expository Dictionary of New Testament Words*, s.v. "abolish," 14.

25. Kenneth S. Wuest, *Hebrews in the Greek New Testament* (Grand Rapids, MI: Wm. B. Eerdmans Publishing Co., 1947), 63-64.

26. Blue Letter Bible, s.v. "*lyō*," accessed September 6, 2019, https://www.blueletterbible.org/lang/lexicon/lexicon .cfm?Strongs=G3089&t=KJV.

27. John A. MacMillan, *The Authority of the Believer* (Camp Hill, PA: WingSpread Publishers, 2007), 21-22.

28. MacMillan, *The Authority of the Believer,* 23.

CHAPTER 11: FAITH IS THE VICTORY

29. Brian Simmons, *Letters of Love from Peter, John, and Jude, The Passion Translation* (Racine, WI: BroadStreet Publishing Group, LLC, 2016), note b, 37.

30. Joseph H. Thayer, *Thayer's Greek-English Lexicon of the New Testament* (Grand Rapids, MI: Baker Book House Co., 1977), s.v. "#950," #1, 99.

31. William Barclay, *The New Testament Volume II, The Letters and the Revelation* (London: Fontana/Collins, 1969).

CHAPTER 12: SECURING THE DESTINIES OF NATIONS

32. H. W. F. Gesenius, *Gesenius' Hebrew-Chaldee Lexicon to the Old Testament* (Grand Rapids, MI: Baker Publishing Group, 1990), s.v. "#7854," #1, 788.

CHAPTER 13: STOP ACCEPTING DELAYS

33. Joseph H. Thayer, *Thayer's Greek-English Lexicon of the New Testament* (Grand Rapids, MI: Baker Book House Co., 1977), s.v. "#5048," #2, 618.

CHAPTER 14: TAKE THE FIRST STEP

34. Thayer, *Thayer's Greek-English Lexicon of the New Testament*, s.v. "#3875," #1, 483.

35. Henderson, *Operating in the Courts of Heaven*, 25-35.

BIBLIOGRAPHY

Ayto, John. *Arcade Dictionary of Word Origins*. New York: Arcade Publishing Company/Little, Brown Company, 1990.

Barclay, William. *The New Testament: A New Translation*. London: Fontana/Collins, 1969.

Gesenius, H. W. F. *Gesenius' Hebrew-Chaldee Lexicon to the Old Testament*. Grand Rapids: Baker Book House, 1990.

Henderson, Robert. *Operating in the Courts of Heaven: Granting God the Legal Right to Fulfill His Passion and Answer our Prayers*. Waco, TX: Robert Henderson Ministries, 2014.

——. *Receiving Healing from the Courts of Heaven: Removing Hinderances that Delay or Deny Healing*. Shippensburg, PA: Destiny Image Publishers, 2018.

——. *Unlocking Destinies from the Courts of Heaven: Dissolving Curses that Delay and Deny Our Futures*. Waco, TX: Robert Henderson Ministries, 2016.

Kenyon, E. W. *New Creation Realities*. Seattle, WA: Kenyon's Gospel Publishing Society, 1945.

Leaf, Caroline. *Switch On Your Brain: The Key to Peak Happiness, Thinking, and Health*. Grand Rapids, MI: Baker Books, 2013.

MacMillan, John A. *The Authority of the Believer.* Camp Hill, PA: WingSpread Publishers, 1981.

Simmons, Brian. *Romans: Grace and Glory, The Passion Translation.* Racine, WI: BroadStreet Publishing Group, LLC, 2015.

————. *Letters of Love: From Peter, John, and Jude, The Passion Translation.* Racine, WI: BroadStreet Publishing Group, LLC, 2016.

Strong, James H. *Strong's Exhaustive Concordance: Complete and Unabridged, Compact Edition with Dictionaries of Hebrew and Greek Words.* Grand Rapids, MI: Baker Book House, 1991.

Thayer, Joseph H. *Thayer's Greek-English Lexicon of the New Testament: A Dictionary Coded to Strong's Exhaustive Concordance.* Grand Rapids, MI: Baker Book House, 1977.

Vine, W. E. *An Expository Dictionary of New Testament Words: With Their Precise Meanings for English Readers.* Old Tappan, NJ: Fleming H. Revell Company, 1966.

Worrell, A. S. *The Worrell New Testament: A. S. Worrell's Translation With Study Notes.* Springfield, MO: Gospel Publishing House, 1980.

Wuest, Kenneth S. *Wuest's Word Studies from the Greek New Testament: For the English Reader, Three-Volume Edition.* Grand Rapids, MI: Wm. B. Eerdmans Publishing Company, 1973.

ABOUT THE AUTHOR

Dr. Bill Dennington has been in full-time ministry for over forty years. He serves the Body of Christ as an apostolic leader and teacher; he has pioneered two churches and ministered in Bible schools, conferences, and churches across the United States and internationally.

Bill has a depth of understanding and revelation of the Word that centers around new creation realities and the finished work of redemption. Always seeking more effective ways to help people reach their full potential in Christ, Bill combines a deep understanding of the laws of faith; the importance of mind renewal; and a functional, practical knowledge of the courts of Heaven that instills spiritual hunger and energy into those who hear him.

Bill is a 1979 graduate of Rhema Bible Training College in Tulsa, Oklahoma. He earned a bachelor's degree and master's degree in theology from Life Christian University near Tampa, Florida and a doctorate in theology from New Life Bible School in Cleveland, Tennessee.

Bill and his wife, Lorie, have been married for thirty-eight years, and have two children and three grandchildren. Bill and Lorie have served as the founding and senior pastors of Harvestfire Church International since 1995.